P9-DDL-674

PSALMS

GENESIS SECTION
Psalms 1—41

J. Vernon McGee

THOMAS NELSON PUBLISHERS

Nashville

Published in Nashville, Tennessee, by Thomas Nelson, Inc.

Scripture quotations are from the KING JAMES VERSION of the Bible.

Library of Congress Cataloging-in-Publication Data

McGee, J. Vernon (John Vernon), 1904–1988
   [Thru the Bible with J. Vernon McGee]
   Thru the Bible commentary series / J. Vernon McGee.
     p.   cm.
   Reprint. Originally published: Thru the Bible with J. Vernon McGee. 1975.
   Includes bibliographical references.
   ISBN 0-7852-1018-0 (TR)
   ISBN 0-8407-3268-6 NRM
   1. Bible—Commentaries. I. Title.
BS491.2.M37 1991
220.7'7—dc20   90–41340
                                  CIP

Printed in the United States of America
13 14 15 16 – 04 03 02 01 00 99

CONTENTS

PSALMS 1—41

PREFACE

The radio broadcasts of the Thru the Bible Radio five-year program were transcribed, edited, and published first in single-volume paperbacks to accommodate the radio audience.

There has been a minimal amount of further editing for this publication. Therefore, these messages are not the word-for-word recording of the taped messages which went out over the air. The changes were necessary to accommodate a reading audience rather than a listening audience.

These are popular messages, prepared originally for a radio audience. They should not be considered a commentary on the entire Bible in any sense of that term. These messages are devoid of any attempt to present a theological or technical commentary on the Bible. Behind these messages is a great deal of research and study in order to interpret the Bible from a popular rather than from a scholarly (and too-often boring) viewpoint.

We have definitely and deliberately attempted "to put the cookies on the bottom shelf so that the kiddies could get them."

The fact that these messages have been translated into many languages for radio broadcasting and have been received with enthusiasm reveals the need for a simple teaching of the whole Bible for the masses of the world.

I am indebted to many people and to many sources for bringing this volume into existence. I should express my special thanks to my secretary, Gertrude Cutler, who supervised the editorial work; to Dr. Elliott R. Cole, my associate, who handled all the detailed work with the publishers; and finally, to my wife Ruth for tenaciously encouraging me from the beginning to put my notes and messages into printed form.

Solomon wrote, ". . . of making many books there is no end; and much study is a weariness of the flesh" (Eccl. 12:12). On a sea of books that flood the marketplace, we launch this series of THRU THE BIBLE with the hope that it might draw many to the one Book, *The Bible.*

J. VERNON MCGEE

The Book of
PSALMS

INTRODUCTION

The title in the Hebrew means *Praises* or *Book of Praises*. The title in the Greek suggests the idea of an instrumental accompaniment. Our title comes from the Greek *psalmos*. It is the book of worship. It is the hymnbook of the temple.

Many writers contributed one or more psalms. David, "the sweet psalmist of Israel," has seventy-three psalms assigned to him. (Psalm 2 is ascribed to him in Acts 4:25; Psalm 95 is ascribed to him in Hebrews 4:7.) Also he could be the author of some of the "Orphanic" psalms. He was peculiarly endowed to write these songs from experience as well as a special aptitude. He arranged those in existence in his day for temple use. The other writers are as follows: Moses, 1 (90th); Solomon, 2; Sons of Korah, 11; Asaph, 12; Heman, 1 (88th); Ethan, 1 (89th); Hezekiah, 10; "Orphanic," 39 (David may be the writer of some of these). There are 150 psalms.

Christ (the Messiah) is prominent throughout. The King and the Kingdom are the theme songs of the Psalms.

The key word in the Book of Psalms is *Hallelujah*, that is, *Praise the Lord*. This phrase has become a Christian cliché, but it is one that should cause a swelling of great emotion in the soul. Hallelujah, praise the Lord!

Psalms 50 and 150 I consider to be the key psalms. Psalm 50, a psalm of Asaph, probably tells more than any other. Psalm 150 is the hallelujah chorus—the word *hallelujah* occurs thirteen times in its six brief verses. It concludes the Book of Psalms and could be considered the chorus of all other psalms.

The Psalms record deep devotion, intense feeling, exalted emotion, and dark dejection. They play upon the keyboard of the human soul with all the stops pulled out. Very candidly, I feel overwhelmed when I come to this marvelous book. It is located in the very center of God's Word. Psalm 119 is in the very center of the Word of God, and it exalts His Word.

This book has blessed the hearts of multitudes down through the ages. When I have been sick at home, or in the hospital, or when some problem is pressing upon my mind and heart, I find myself always turning to the Psalms. They always bless my heart and life. Apparently down through the ages it has been that way. Ambrose, one of the great saints of the church, said, "The Psalms are the voices of the church." Augustine said, "They are the epitome of the whole Scripture." Martin Luther said, "They are a little book for all saints." John Calvin said, "They are the anatomy of all parts of the soul." I like that.

Someone has said that there are 126 psychological experiences—I don't know how they arrived at that number—but I do know that all of them are recorded in the Book of Psalms. It is the *only* book which contains every experience of a human being. The Psalms run the psychological gamut. Every thought, every impulse, every emotion that sweeps over the soul is recorded in this book. That is the reason, I suppose, that it always speaks to our hearts and finds a responsive chord wherever we turn.

Hooker said of the Psalms, "They are the choice and flower of all things profitable in other books." Donne put it this way, "The Psalms foretell what I, what any, shall do and suffer and say." Herd called the Psalms, "A hymnbook for all time." Watts said, "They are the thousand-voiced heart of the church." The place Psalms have held in the lives of God's people testifies to their universality, although they have a peculiar Jewish application. They express the deep feelings of all believing hearts in all generations.

The Psalms are full of Christ. There is a more complete picture of Him in the Psalms than in the Gospels. The Gospels tell us that He went to the mountain to pray, but the Psalms give us His prayer. The

Gospels tell us that He was crucified, but the Psalms tell us what went on in His own heart during the Crucifixion. The Gospels tell us He went back to heaven, but the Psalms begin where the Gospels leave off and show us Christ seated in heaven.

Christ the Messiah is prominent throughout this book. You will remember that the Lord Jesus, when He appeared after His resurrection to those who were His own, said to them, ". . . These are the words which I spake unto you, while I was yet with you, that all things must be fulfilled, which were written in the law of Moses, and in the prophets, and in the psalms, concerning me" (Luke 24:44). Christ is the subject of the Psalms. I think He is the object of praise in every one of them. I will not be able to locate Him in every one of them, but that does not mean that He is not in each psalm; it only means that Vernon McGee is limited. Although all of them have Christ as the object of worship, some are technically called messianic psalms. These record the birth, life, death, resurrection, glory, priesthood, kingship, and return of Christ. There are sixteen messianic psalms that speak specifically about Christ, but as I have already said, all 150 of them are about Him. The Book of Psalms is a hymnbook and a HIM book—it is all about Him. As we study it, that fact will become very clear.

In a more restrictive sense, the Psalms deal with Christ belonging to Israel and Israel belonging to Christ. Both themes are connected to the rebellion of man. There is no blessing on this earth until Israel and Christ are brought together. The Psalms are Jewish in expectation and hope. They are songs which were adapted to temple worship. That does not mean, however, that they do not have a spiritual application and interpretation for us today. They certainly do. I probably turn to them more than to any other portion of the Word of God, but we need to be a little more exacting in our interpretation of the Psalms. For example, God is not spoken of as a Father in this book. The saints are not called sons. In the Psalms He is God the Father, not the Father God. The abiding presence of the Holy Spirit and the blessed hope of the New Testament are not in this book. Failure to recognize this has led many people astray in their interpretation of Psalm 2. The reference in this song is not to the rapture of the church but to the second coming of Christ to the earth to establish His kingdom and to reign in Jerusalem.

The imprecatory psalms have caused the most criticism because of their vindictiveness and prayers for judgment. These psalms came from a time of war and from a people who under law were looking for justice and peace on earth. My friend, you cannot have peace without putting down unrighteousness and rebellion. Apparently God intends to do just that, and He makes no apology for it. In His own time He will move in judgment upon this earth. In the New Testament the Christian is told to love his enemies, and it may startle you to read prayers in the Psalms that say some very harsh things about the enemy. But judgment is to bring justice upon this earth. Also there are psalms that anticipate the period when Antichrist will be in power. We have no reasonable basis to dictate how people should act or what they should pray under such circumstances.

Other types of psalms include the penitential, historic, nature, pilgrim, Hallel, missionary, puritan, acrostic, and praise of God's Word. This is a rich section we are coming to. We are going to mine for gold and diamonds here, my friend.

The Book of Psalms is not arranged in a haphazard sort of way. Some folk seem to think that the Psalms were dropped into a tub, shaken up, then put together with no arrangement. However, it is interesting to note that one psalm will state a principle, then there will follow several psalms that will be explanatory. Psalms 1—8 are an example of this.

The Book of Psalms is arranged in an orderly manner. In fact, it has been noted for years that the Book of Psalms is arranged and corresponds to the Pentateuch of Moses. There are Genesis, Exodus, Leviticus, Numbers, and Deuteronomy sections, as you will see in the outline which follows.

The correspondence between the Psalms and the Pentateuch is easily seen. For instance, in the Genesis section you see the perfect man in a state of blessedness, as in Psalm 1. Next you have the fall and recovery of man in view. Psalm 2 pictures the rebellious man. In Psalm 3 is the perfect man rejected. In Psalm 4 we see the conflict between the seed of the woman and the serpent. In Psalm 5 we find the perfect man in the midst of enemies. Psalm 6 presents the perfect man in the midst of chastisement with the bruising of his heel. In Psalm 7 we see the perfect man in the midst of false witnesses. Finally, in Psalm 8 we see the salvation of man coming through the bruising of the head. In Psalms 9—15 we see the enemy and Antichrist conflict and the final deliverance. Then in Psalms 16—41 we see Christ in the midst of His people sanctifying them to God. All of this will be seen as we go through the Book of Psalms.

Spurgeon said, "The Book of Psalms instructs us in the use of wings as well as words. It sets us both mounting and singing." This is the book that may make a skylark out of you instead of some other kind of a bird. This book has been called the epitome and analogy of the soul. It has also been designated as the garden of the Scriptures. Out of 219 quotations of the Old Testament in the New Testament, 116 of them are from the Psalms. You will see 150 spiritual songs which undoubtedly at one time were all set to music. This is a book which ought to make our hearts sing.

OUTLINE

I. Genesis Section, Psalms 1—41
Man seen in a state of blessedness, fall, and recovery (Man in View)
- A. Perfect Man (Last Adam), Psalm 1
- B. Rebellious Man, Psalm 2
- C. Perfect Man Rejected, Psalm 3
- D. Conflict between Seed of Woman and Serpent, Psalm 4
- E. Perfect Man in Midst of Enemies, Psalm 5
- F. Perfect Man in Midst of Chastisement (Bruising Heel), Psalm 6
- G. Perfect Man in Midst of False Witnesses, Psalm 7
- H. Repair of Man Comes through Man (Bruising Head), Psalm 8
- I. Enemy and Antichrist Conflict; Final Deliverance, Psalms 9—15
- J. Christ in Midst of His People Sanctifying Them to God, Psalms 16—41

II. Exodus Section, Psalms 42—72
Ruin and Redemption (Israel in View)
- A. Israel's Ruin, Psalms 42—49
- B. Israel's Redeemer, Psalms 50—60
- C. Israel's Redemption, Psalms 61—72

III. Leviticus Section, Psalms 73—89
Darkness and dawn (Sanctuary in View)
Tabernacle, temple, house, assembly and congregation in almost every psalm.

IV. Numbers Section, Psalms 90—106
Peril and protection (Earth in View)

V. Deuteronomy Section, Psalms 107—150
Perfection and praise of the Word of God

PSALM 1

THEME: Two men, two ways, two destinies

This is the psalm which opens the Genesis section. It begins with man instead of the material universe. This psalm talks about the blessed man, or the happy man. The blessed man is contrasted to the ungodly. It is also a picture of Christ, the last Adam, in the midst of ungodly sinners and the scornful. We sometimes think of the Lord as a man of sorrows and acquainted with grief, and for some strange reason many of the pictures that have been painted of Him reveal Him as a very sad-looking individual. It is true that Isaiah says He is a Man of Sorrows, but why don't you read on? In Isaiah you will find that Christ did not have any sorrows and griefs of His own. Isaiah 53:4 says, "Surely he hath borne our griefs, and carried our sorrows: yet we did esteem him stricken, smitten of God, and afflicted." It was our griefs, not His own, that He was carrying. He was the happy Christ. This is a picture of Him.

PRACTICE OF THE BLESSED MAN

Blessed is the man that walketh not in the counsel of the ungodly, nor standeth in the way of sinners, nor sitteth in the seat of the scornful [Ps. 1:1].

This verse states the *practice* of the blessed man. A little bit further in this psalm we will see the *power* of the blessed man, and finally his *permanency*. In this first verse we see the negative side of the practice of the blessed man. We are told what the happy man does *not* do. Here we see three positions or postures. Blessed is the man, or happy is the man, who does not walk in the counsel of the ungodly, nor stand in the way of sinners, nor sit in the seat of the scornful. The person who does these things is not a happy person. He goes through three stages.

First he associates with the ungodly, then he gets in with sinners, and finally he joins in with the scornful.

There is definitely regression, deterioration, and degeneration here. The blessed man does not walk in the counsel of the ungodly. *Counsel* means "advice." He does not listen to the ungodly. Have you ever noticed that even the Lord Jesus never referred to His own reason or His own mind as the basis for a decision? Whatever He did was based on the will of God. He never said to His disciples, "Fellows, we are going into Galilee again. I have been thinking this over, and I am smarter than you fellows, and I think this is the best thing to do according to my point of view." That is not the way He approached His disciples. He always said, "I am going to Jerusalem because it is the will of my Father." He spent time with His Father and knew what His will was and moved into certain areas on that basis.

My friend, it is one thing to listen to counsel, and good counsel is fine, but certainly not the counsel of the ungodly. We are to walk by faith. Listening to the counsel of the ungodly is not walking by faith. Who are the ungodly? They are the people who just leave God out. There is no fear of God before their eyes. They live as though God does not exist. Around us today are multitudes of people like this. They get up in the morning, never turn to God in prayer, never thank Him for the food they eat or for life or health. They just keep moving right along, living it up. They are ungodly—they just leave God out.

The ungodly counsels the man, and now we find him standing in the way of sinners. It is the sinner who takes him from there. Sin means to "miss the mark." They don't quite live as they should. They are the ones the Scripture speaks of when it says, "There is a way which seemeth right unto a man, but the end thereof are the ways of death" (Prov. 14:12). Again the Scriptures say, "All the ways of a man are clean in his own eyes . . ." (Prov. 16:2). The sinner may think he is all right, but he is a *sinner*. God's Word says, "Let the wicked forsake his way, and the unrighteous man his thoughts . . ." (Isa. 55:7). Also it says, "All we like sheep have gone astray; we have turned every one to his own way; and the Lord hath laid on him the iniquity of us all" (Isa. 53:6). The Father laid on the Lord Jesus all the weight of our guilt. We are sinners. That's our picture.

The next step down from standing in the way of sinners is sitting in the seat of the scornful. The scorners are atheists. Now the sinner gets the young man to sit down. We are told that the third stage is that he sits in the seat of the scornful. The scornful is the atheist. He not only denies God, but he exhibits an antagonism and a hatred of God. This we see on every hand today. The scornful—they're the ones who are absolutely opposed to God. They don't want the Bible read in the public schools; they don't want it read anywhere for that matter. They deny the Word of God. May I say to you that there is nothing lower than to deny God. The drunkard in the gutter today is not nearly as low as the man who is denying God. And if you want to know God's attitude, here it is: "Surely he scorneth the scorners: but he giveth grace unto the lowly" (Prov. 3:34). God is opposed to the scornful, and He will scorn them. That's a very frightful picture, by the way, presented here.

Now this is the negative side. This is what the happy man does not do. In the next verse we see what the happy man *does* do.

But his delight is in the law of the Lord; and in his law doth he meditate day and night [Ps. 1:2].

You remember our Lord told about a man possessed with a demon, and when the demon went out of him the man cleaned up his life. He was swept and garnished—he had a new paint job. He was all cleaned up and he thought he was all right. But that demon still owned him. The demon wandered around, got tired of traveling, and returned. When he came back he brought some friends with him—seven other spirits more wicked than himself. And we're told that the last estate of the man was worse than the first. Many folk think that if they clean up their lives a little, that is all that is necessary. But notice, "his delight is in the law of the Lord." The delight of God's man is in the law of the Lord. In other words, he finds joy in the Word of God. I wish I could get the message over to folk that the Bible is a thrilling Book. It's not a burden; it's not boring. It is real delight to read and study the Word of God. Blessed is the man—*happy* is the man—whose delight is in the law of the Lord. Today the tragedy that has come to man—the tear, the sigh, the groaning, the heartache, the heartbreak, the broken homes, the ruined and wrecked lives—are the result of God's broken laws. The Word of God makes it very clear. "For this is the love of God, that we keep his commandments: and his commandments are not grievous" (1 John 5:3). His commandments for believers today are not only the Ten Commandments. And His commandments are not burdensome.

The idea that being saved by grace means that you can be lawless and live as you please is not the picture given to us in the Word of God. We are not to be lawless. "For, brethren, ye have been called unto liberty; only use not liberty for an occasion to the flesh, but by love serve one another" (Gal. 5:13). Liberty is not license by any means. Of course we don't keep the Ten Commandments to be saved, but that doesn't mean we are to break them. It means, my friend, that you cannot measure up to God's law. He demands perfection, and you and I don't have it. We have to come to God by faith. After we are saved by faith, we are to live on a higher plane than the law. We are to have in our lives the fruit of the Spirit, which is: love, joy, peace, long-suffering, gentleness, goodness, faithfulness, meekness, and self-control. We have the discipline and guidance of grace.

"His delight is in the law of the Lord; and in his law doth he meditate." *Meditate* is a very figurative word. It pictures a cow chewing her cud. I'm told that the cow has several compartments in her tummy. She can go out in the morning, graze on the grass when the dew is on it in the cool of the day. Then when it gets hot in the middle of the day, she lies down under a tree and begins to chew the cud. She moves the grass she had in the morning back up and now she masticates it, she goes over it again. That is what we do when we meditate. We go over what we have read. Thomas á Kempis put it rather quaintly: "I have no rest, but in a nook, with the Book." Way back in 1688 Bartholomew Ashwood said, "Meditation chews the cud." My, how that is needed today in the lives of believers. Remember that James spoke of the man who beholds his natural face in a mirror, then ". . . straightway forgetteth what manner of man he was" (James 1:24). We are to meditate on the Word of God (which is God's mirror that shows us what we really are). We are to allow the Word to shape our lives.

"And in his law doth he meditate day and night." My friend, God has no plan or program by which you are to grow and develop as a believer apart from His Word. You can become as busy as a termite in your church (and possibly with the same effect as a termite), but you won't grow by means of activity. You will grow by meditating upon the Word of God—that is, by going over it again and again in your thinking until it becomes a part of your life. This is the practice of the happy man.

POWER OF THE BLESSED MAN

Where does he get his power?

And he shall be like a tree planted by the rivers of water, that bringeth forth his fruit in his season; his leaf also shall not wither; and whatsoever he doeth shall prosper [Ps. 1:3].

The happy man shall be like a tree planted by the rivers of water. The word *rivers* is the superlative in the Hebrew; it is a hyperbole for *abundance*. The blessed man is planted, given plenty of water, and becomes a tree. God's trees are "planted" trees. They are not wild-growing trees by any means. I think this picture refers to being born again. Isaiah 61:3 says, "To appoint unto them that mourn in Zion, to give unto them beauty for ashes, the oil of joy for mourning, the garment of praise for the spirit of heaviness; that they might be called *trees* of righteousness, the *planting* of the LORD, that he might be glorified." God does not use wild-grown trees. His trees are born again, taken up and set out in God's garden—set out by the rivers of water.

What does "rivers of water" mean? That is the Word of God. Somebody asks, "Are you sure about that?" Oh, I *know* it, because Isaiah 55:10–11 tells me, "For as the rain cometh down, and the snow from heaven, and returneth not thither, but watereth the earth, and maketh it bring forth and bud, that it may give seed to the sower, and bread to the eater: So shall my *word* be that goeth forth out of my mouth: it shall not return unto me void, but it shall accomplish that which I please, and it shall prosper in the thing whereto I sent it." God wants His Word to come down like rain. The radio is a fine way to do this—it scatters God's Word everywhere. We are to get out the Word of God. And it will produce something—it will cause trees to grow.

It provides drink and sustenance. It is also cleansing, and you can see this washing of water with the Word expressed by the psalmist in Psalm 104:16, which says, "The trees of the Lord are full of sap; the cedars of Lebanon, which he hath planted." Now the psalmist does not say that God's trees are *saps*, he says that they are full of sap. That "sap" is the Word of God—the trees of Lebanon which He has planted are full of the Word of God.

Each tree "bringeth forth his fruit in his season." It is interesting to note that God's trees don't bring forth fruit all of the time. They bring forth in their season, and the power is in the Word of God. I have heard the statement made in this day of activity and nervous action that the primary business of a Christian is soul-winning. I disagree with that. The Word of God does not say it. Second Corinthians 2:14–16 says, "Now thanks be unto God, which always causeth us to triumph in Christ, and maketh manifest the savour of his knowledge by us in every place. For we are unto God a sweet savour of Christ, in them that are saved, and in them that perish: To the one we are the savour of death unto death; and to the other the savour of life unto life. And who is sufficient for these things?" Well, I am not, but I do know this: I am called to give out the Word of God. It is the business of the Holy Spirit to bring people to Christ. We are experiencing multitudes of people coming to Christ through our radio program. I am amazed at it, but *we* don't do it. We just give out the Word of God, and when we do, our God causes us to triumph. Suppose nobody accepted Christ? Then we are a savour of life to those who are saved and a savour of death to those who perish. My responsibility is to give you the Word of God, and it is your responsibility to do something about it. When I was a pastor, I used to tell folk when I gave an invitation to receive Christ, "If you leave here unsaved, it's too bad because you can't go into God's presence saying you had not heard the Gospel. I really have become your enemy because you cannot tell God that you had never heard His Word." It is your business to give it to the unsaved, my friend, and it is his business what he does with it. But he will have to be accountable to God. God tells us to get out the Word of God, and that is what I've been trying to do for many years. Some are saved, and some are not saved.

At Dr. George Truett's fiftieth anniversary as pastor of the First Baptist Church of Dallas, Texas, a very prominent lawyer came up to him after the morning service. He said, "George, you and I came to Dallas in the early days, in the horse-and-buggy days. I want to make a confession to you. As a young lawyer, I used to come in to hear you. You were a young preacher in those days, but you disturbed me. Many a time I went home after a Sunday night service and I couldn't sleep." But he said, "George, today you have become the greatest preacher in America, but I can sit and listen to you now, and you don't bother me at all." And he laughed and walked away.

I'd hate to be that lawyer. As brilliant as he is, he won't have much of a case to offer when he stands before Christ someday because he happened to have listened to one of the greatest preachers America ever produced. Dr. Truett was called the prince of the pulpit. For fifty years that lawyer listened to him. And at the end of fifty years he said, "You don't bother me at all." But Dr. Truett had discharged his responsibility.

The primary business of a Christian is not soul-winning, but getting out the Word of God, my friend. It "bringeth forth his fruit in his season." There is a time to get fruit. I have a little tangerine tree that overdid itself one year. It was loaded with tangerines. I know I picked two bushels off that tree, and there still were two more bushels there. But a month later there wasn't one tangerine on that tree. It only brings forth its fruit in its season. There is a season for fruitbearing. That is the reason there ought to be a long time of preparation, of sowing seed, of helping it to fructify. Just to hand out a tract here and there may have its value, but, my friend, we are in the business of giving out the living Word of God, and it needs to be tended. It takes time and care because fruit comes forth only at the right season.

He also says: "His leaf also shall not wither." Now the leaf is the outward testimony of the Christian. That is something that should be out all the time. God's trees are evergreens—they never lose their testimony. A friend of mine, while taking a course at a seminary in New York one summer, went to one of those famous churches in New York City one Sunday. He said, "I walked down on Sunday morning to this great church and saw over the entrance, carved in stone, these words: The Gate of Heaven. Then I saw underneath it a temporary sign: Closed During July and August." Too often this happens in the lives of individual believers, but it should not, my friend. You are always an evergreen. Your leaf is the outward testimony that you have in this world for Christ. All God's children are evergreens.

In addition to this he says, "whatsoever he doeth shall prosper." Back in the Old Testament God promised material blessings to His own. Those blessings are not promised to the believer today. If you have them, you can thank Him for more than He has promised. John Trapp put it like this: "Outward prosperity, if it follows close walking with God, is sweet. As the cipher when it follows a figure adds to the number, though it be nothing by itself." The important thing is to have Christ. That's number one. All material blessings are zero. If you don't have One before your zeroes, you have only a goose egg, friend. But if you put that One, who is Christ, before your material blessings, then you are blessed indeed. But remember that He has not promised material blessings in this age.

PERMANENCY OF THE BLESSED MAN

Notice the insecurity of the ungodly.

> **The ungodly are not so: but are like the chaff which the wind driveth away.**
>
> **Therefore the ungodly shall not stand in the judgment, nor sinners in the congregation of the righteous [Ps. 1:4–5].**

Two men, two ways, two destinies. One is a dead-end street; it leads to death. The other leads to life. God says what is right and what is wrong. We are living in a day when folk are not sure what is right or wrong. God is sure. His Word does not change with every philosophy of a new generation.

For the LORD knoweth the way of the righteous: but the way of the ungodly shall perish [Ps. 1:6].

Perish simply means "lost." It is a word of finality, if you please. The wicked are going to perish; Proverbs 10:28 tells us: "The hope of the righteous shall be gladness: but the expectation of the wicked shall perish." We are admonished: "Enter ye in at the strait gate: for wide is the gate, and broad is the way, that leadeth to destruction, and many there be which go in thereat: because strait is the gate, and narrow is the way, which leadeth unto life, and few there be that find it" (Matt. 7:13–14). The wide, broad way is like a funnel in that you enter at the big end and, as you continue, it becomes narrower and narrower and finally leads to death. You enter the narrow way by Christ, who is the way, the truth, and the life. As you continue, the way becomes broader and broader; and this way leads to life. In John 10:10 Christ says, ". . . I am come that they might have life, and that they might have it more abundantly." What a glorious picture of the blessed and happy man is presented in the first psalm!

PSALM 2

THEME: *Drama of the ages—man's rebellion against God*

A noticeable feature in the Book of Psalms is the systematic arrangement. The first psalm presents the perfect man, the happy man. (And I believe it pictures the Lord Jesus Christ as the last Adam.) Now in contrast to the perfect man, the blessed man in Psalm 1, we see the rebellious man in Psalm 2. We call this the Genesis section of the Book of Psalms, and the parallel is striking. Genesis begins with the perfect man, the happy man, in the Garden of Eden. But he became the rebellious man who ran away from God, was no longer seeking Him, who had no capacity for Him. Now here in Psalm 2 we find the children of Adam—mankind.

Psalm 2 has been called the drama of the ages. It contains a decisive declaration concerning the outcome of events and forces that are in the world today. This psalm is divided more like a television program than a play. It is presented as if there was a camera on earth and one in heaven. We experienced something like this when we were treated to on-the-spot moon exploration by camera. It was quite exciting and dramatic.

When we come to the second psalm we find that the Spirit of God uses two cameras in a dramatic way beyond the imagination of man. First, the camera on earth comes on, and when it does, we hear the voices of the masses. We hear little man speaking his little piece and playing his part—as Shakespeare puts it, "A poor player that struts and frets his hour upon the stage" of life. Little man. Then the camera on earth goes off, the camera in heaven comes on, and we hear God the Father speak. After He speaks, the camera shifts to His right hand, and God the Son speaks His part. Then the camera in heaven goes off, the camera on earth comes on again, and God the Holy Spirit has the last word.

CAMERA FOCUS: MANKIND

Now let's watch this presentation. First, the camera on earth comes on, and we see mankind. He is put before us here in the first verse with this question:

Why do the heathen rage, and the people imagine a vain thing? [Ps. 2:1].

Why do the heathen (Gentiles) rage, and the people (Jews) imagine a vain thing? The word *vain* here means "empty." It means that this which has so enraged the Gentiles, and which has brought together mankind in a great mass movement, a great protest movement, will never be fulfilled, will never be accomplished. It is an empty, futile thing that has brought mankind together.

Well, what is it?

The kings of the earth set themselves, and the rulers take counsel together, against the Lord, and against his anointed, saying [Ps. 2:2].

"The kings of the earth set themselves" are the political rulers, "and the rulers take counsel together" are the religious rulers. Not only do you have the masses of mankind in this protest movement, but also the establishment has joined in with it. Here are the rulers, both religious and political, joining together.

Now what is it they are protesting? Whom are they against? "Against the Lord, and against his anointed." The word *anointed* here means "Messiah"—that is what it is in Hebrew. When the word is brought over in the Greek New Testament it is *Christos,* and in English "Christ." Here is a great worldwide movement that is against God and against Christ.

Now when did this movement begin? Scripture lets us know about this. Over in the fourth chapter of the Book of Acts, when the first persecution broke out against the church, we're told that the apostles, Peter and John, after they had been threatened, returned back to the church to give their report: "And when they heard that, they lifted up their voice to God with one accord, and said, Lord, thou art God . . ." (Acts 4:24).

We need to pause here just a moment because this is one of the things the church is not sure about today: "Lord, thou art God." Many people are not sure He is God. They wonder. The early church had no misgivings or questions.

". . . Lord, thou art God, which hast made heaven, and earth, and the sea, and all that in them is: Who by the mouth of thy servant David hast said, Why did the heathen rage, and the people imagine vain things?" (Acts 4:24–25). As you can see, they were quoting Psalm 2. "The kings of the earth stood up, and the rulers were gathered together against the Lord, and against his Christ" (Acts 4:26). Now this is the Holy Spirit's interpretation: "For of a truth against thy holy child Jesus, whom thou hast anointed, both Herod, and Pontius Pilate, with the Gentiles, and the people of Israel, were gathered together" (Acts 4:27). Here is this movement, beginning, we are told by the Holy Spirit, back yonder when Pilate joined up with the religious rulers and Herod in order to put Jesus to death. This is a movement against God and Christ. It has been snowballing as it has come down through the centuries, and it will break out finally in a worldwide revolution against God and against Christ.

Now somebody says to me, "You really don't think the world is moving in that direction, do you?" May I say to you, I think it is. Someone comes to me and asks, "Dr. McGee, do you think the world is getting better?" I say, "Yes, I do." Somebody else comes and says, "Dr. McGee, don't you think the world is getting worse?" I say, "Yes, I do." "Well," you may say, "what in the world are you trying to do? Go with both crowds?" No, both are true. That is the same thing the Lord Jesus said in His parable of the tares (Matt. 13:24–39). The Lord Jesus said that He Himself is the sower and that He is sowing seed in the world. Then He said an enemy came in and sowed tares. The servants wanted to go in and pull up the tares. When I entered the ministry that is what I wanted to do. I was the best puller-upper of tares you've ever seen. But I soon found out that we're not called to pull up tares (I sure found that out the hard way!). That is the reason I don't try to straighten out anybody else. I'm having enough trouble with Vernon McGee, so I don't worry about the others. He will take care of them. But what He said was that the wheat is growing, the tares are growing, they are both growing together, and He will do the separating. He will take care of that.

Today the good is growing. Did you know that there is more Bible teaching going out today than in any period in the history of the world? We brag about the few radio stations that carry our Bible study, but other radio programs have been giving out the Word lots longer than we have. Across this land are many radio stations that are dedicated to the ministry of broadcasting the Word of God. The Word is going out today through many more avenues than it has ever gone out before. The wheat is growing. But I want to tell you, brother, the tares are growing also. Evil is growing. There is an opposition against God and Christ today that is unbelievable. I could give you many incidents of the enmity that I've encountered.

Somebody says, "I just can't quite buy that. I believe that over there on the other side of the Iron Curtain atheism is growing, but not on this side." Well, it is growing on the other side, and it is rather amazing. Did you know that you and I have seen in our lifetime (those of you who are as old as I am) a nation appear whose basic philosophy, basic political economy, is atheism? There has been nothing like that in the past. No nation of the ancient world, that great pagan world of the past, was atheistic. Not one. Somebody says, "I thought they were." No, they were the opposite. They were polytheistic. They worshiped many gods. None was atheistic. You see, they were too close to the mooring mast of revelation. Noah knew a man who knew Adam. When you are that close to it, you do not deny God. In Noah's day the world was filled with violence, but there wasn't an atheist in the crowd. When God gave the Ten Commandments, He didn't give any one of them against atheism. He gave two against polytheism: "Thou shalt have no other gods before me. Thou shalt not make unto thee any graven image, or any likeness of any thing that is in heaven above, or that is in the earth beneath, or that is in the water under the earth" (Exod. 20:3–4). He gave these two commandments against polytheism, none against atheism. Why? There were no atheists.

Now when you get to the time of David, you meet atheists, and there were a great many atheists by that time. David labels them, though. He says, "The *fool* hath said in his heart, There is no God . . ." (Ps. 14:1). The word *fool* in the Hebrew means "insane." The insane, the nutty individual, is the one who is the atheist. Of course he may be a Ph.D in a university. The Bible says he is insane. It is insane for a man to say there is no God.

There is, I believe, as much opposition to Jesus Christ on this side of the Iron Curtain as there is on the other side of the Iron Curtain today. I believe that with all my heart. Somebody says, "Wait a minute. I hear many talk about Jesus, and how wonderful Jesus is." Have you ever stopped to think that the Jesus of liberalism, the Jesus the world thinks of, actually never lived? The Jesus of the Bible and the Jesus of liberalism are two different individuals. And the Jesus of liberalism never lived at all.

Let me give you an example of what I mean. For many years when I was a pastor in downtown Los Angeles, the leading liberal in this country pastored a church nearby. Actually I had great respect for him because he was one liberal who was honest. For instance, he would just come out and say he did not believe in the virgin birth. And if you don't believe it, I'd like for you to say it and not beat around the bush. He had a question-and-answer program on radio. I had a question-and-answer program on radio, and listeners would feed questions to both of us to set us in opposition. Every year we went through that same little ritual during the Christmas season. I always enjoyed it. So one time we both were invited to a banquet, and (I think it was done purposely) we were seated together. I got there first and sat down. I saw his name there. In a minute he came in. I felt somebody put his arm around me and say, "You know, Brother McGee, you and I ought to be much closer together. We preach the same Jesus," and he sat down. I said to him, "Are you sure we preach the same Jesus?" "Oh, don't we?" "I don't think so. Let me ask you some questions. Was the Jesus you preach virgin born?" "Of course not." "Well, the one I preach is virgin born. The Jesus you preach—did He perform miracles?" "I do not believe in miracles." "Well, the Jesus I preach performed miracles. The Jesus you preach—did He die on a cross for the sins of the world?" "Of course He died on a cross, but not for the sins of the world." "The Jesus I preach died a substitutionary, vicarious death for the sins of man. Do you believe that Jesus rose bodily?" "Oh, no, of course not." "Obviously then, you and I are not preaching about the same Jesus. Now I want to ask you a question." You see, these liberal men have called some of us fundamentalists "intellectual obscurantists." (Now whatever that is, it's terrible!) So I said to him, "Look, what are the documents or where are the documents for the Jesus you preach?" He laughed, just laughed and passed it off. "Of course we don't have any." "Now isn't that interesting. We have documents for the Jesus we preach, and you don't—yet you call us intellectual obscurantists. I'd like to know who is an intellectual obscurantist!"

May I say to you, my friend, the Jesus that the world believes in today doesn't even exist. He never lived. The Jesus we preach is the Jesus of the Bible, and that is the One against whom there is opposition in the world today. There is a tremendous build-up, a mighty crescendo of opposition against God and against Christ in this day in which we live.

Now how does it manifest itself? Exactly as He said it would. Notice again the second psalm. Hear what they are saying:

Let us break their bands asunder, and cast away their cords from us [Ps. 2:3].

What are some of the bands God has put on the human family? Marriage is one. God has made marriage for the welfare of mankind. Whether you are a Christian or not, God has given marriage to mankind. Today they not only *want* to get rid of it; they *are* getting rid of it. I was rather shocked two or three years ago. (I'm a square. I'm not really keeping up with it today, so I don't follow along in the way they are going in this modern thinking, relative to God, relative to man, and relative to the Word of God.) So I was startled at a young people's conference when the sweetest little girl got up in our question-and-answer period and said, "Dr. McGee, why does a young couple have to get married if they love each other? Why can't they just start living together?" God gave marriage, and God intends for it to be followed. But they say, "Let's break their bands asunder."

Also, "Let's cast away their cords from us." The Ten Commandments are cords. When somebody accuses me of saying that we don't need the Ten Commandments, they are wrong. We are not saved by keeping them—I tried it, and it won't work—but I'll say this: God gave them, and He gave them to protect mankind. They are thrown out the door today, and right now we are experiencing lawlessness in this country because of the fact that crime is not being punished. There has been a terrible toll of lives that would not have been sacrificed had laws been enforced. You see, we are living in a day when the prevailing philosophy is "Let us break their bands asunder, let's cast away their cords from us. We want to be free and do as we please." God says we can't make it that way. It won't work. We've got old evil natures that need to be restrained. But mankind is moving toward getting rid of all restraints today.

It is disturbing as we look at this world in which we are living. In the political world there is confusion. In the moral realm there is corruption. In the spiritual sphere there is compromise and indifference. And in the social sphere there is comfort. This affluent society never had it so easy, and their goal is to make it easier. We are living in that kind of a day. It is disturbing, and I'll be honest with you, I do worry about it a little.

CAMERA FOCUS: GOD THE FATHER

The question arises, How does *God* feel about this?

> **He that sitteth in the heavens shall laugh: the Lord shall have them in derision [Ps. 2:4].**

What kind of laughter is this? Let me say at the outset that it is not the laughter of humor. He is not being funny.

Do not misunderstand me—there is humor in the Bible. The devil has really hit a home run by making people think that going to church is quite an ordeal. We are living in a day when folk think you can't have fun in church. I think the Bible is full of humor. Those of you who study with us through the Bible know we find a lot of it. There used to be a dear maiden lady at a church I served who never found any humor in the Bible. When I gave a message which cited some humorous incident, she used to come down, shake a bony finger under my nose and say, "Dr. McGee, you are being irreverent to find humor in the Bible." I said to her, "Don't you wish you could?" She's gone now to be with the Lord, and I certainly hope she's had a good laugh since she has been there because she has gone to the place where she can have a good time. She needs to have a good time—she never had one down here. There are too many Christians like that today. My friend, it is going to be thrilling to be with Him some day. We're going to have a wonderful time with Him. It's going to be fun, and I'm looking forward to that. God has a sense of humor, and there is humor in His Word.

"He that sitteth in the heavens shall laugh . . ." Since this is not the laughter of humor, what is it? Well, look at it from God's viewpoint—little man down there parading up and down, shaking his midget fist in Heaven's face and saying, "Come on out and fight me! I'm against you." God looks down at the puny little creature. It's utterly *preposterous*. It is so ridiculous! He looks down and laughs. "He that sitteth in the heavens shall laugh: the LORD shall have them in derision." It is so utterly ridiculous, my friend. Little men putting themselves in opposition to God won't be around very long. Mussolini did a lot of talking, and we haven't heard from him lately. Stalin did the same thing, and he is gone. Little man plays his brief role here on the stage of life, then his part is over. How ridiculous and preposterous for him to oppose God!

Then shall he speak unto them in his wrath, and vex them in his sore displeasure [Ps. 2:5].

This is the judgment that is coming upon this earth.

What effect will man's opposition have upon God's program? God is going forward to the accomplishment of His purpose. What little man does down here won't deter Him, detour Him, or defer Him at all. God did not read something in the morning paper that He didn't already know about. There is nothing that has surprised Him at all. He is moving according to His purpose. He has, I believe, a twofold purpose in this world. I think He has a heavenly purpose; I think He has an earthly purpose. Right now He is working on His heavenly purpose. The writer to the Hebrews expresses this: it is ". . . bringing many sons unto glory . . ." (Heb. 2:10). God today is calling out of this world a people to His name. That is His present purpose. However, God has another purpose, and it is stated here:

> **Yet have I set my king upon my holy hill of Zion [Ps. 2:6].**

God is moving forward today undeviatingly, unhesitatingly, uncompromisingly to the establishment of that throne on which Jesus Christ will sit on this earth. I hear folk say, "If the Lord delay His coming." Where in the world did that idea come from? He is not delaying anything. He is going to come on schedule—*His* schedule, not mine, because I don't know when He is coming. He is running on schedule and nothing will stop Him, nothing can cause Him to change His plan.

CAMERA FOCUS: GOD THE SON

Now the camera in heaven shifts to God the Son on His right hand. God the Son speaks, "I will declare the decree." Those of you who have studied theology know that the Lord Jesus executes all the decrees of God.

> **I will declare the decree: the LORD hath said unto me, Thou art my Son; this day have I begotten thee [Ps. 2:7].**

This is a verse that the Jehovah's Witnesses use a great deal. I wish they would listen long enough to find out what it means. It would help them a great deal to find it has no reference to the birth of the Lord Jesus Christ—which they would see if only they would turn to the New Testament and let the Spirit of God interpret. This verse was quoted by the apostle Paul when he preached in Antioch of Pisidia. This was, I believe, one of his greatest sermons; and he was talking about the resurrection of Jesus Christ: "God hath fulfilled the same unto us their children, in that he hath raised up Jesus again; as it is also written in the second psalm, Thou art my Son, this day have I begotten thee" (Acts 13:33).

The reference in the second psalm is not to the *birth* of Jesus. He never was begotten in the sense of having a beginning. Rather, this is in reference to His *resurrection*. Christ was begotten out of Joseph's tomb. Jesus is the eternal Son of God, and God is the eternal Father. You cannot have an eternal Father without having an eternal Son. They were this throughout eternity. This is their position in the Trinity. It hasn't anything to do with someone being born, but it does have something to do with someone being begotten from the dead. It has to do with resurrection. I'm afraid the Jehovah's Witnesses have not heard this, but they could find, with a little honest searching, that the New Testament makes it very clear Jesus Christ is not a creature. He is the theanthropic Person. He is the God-man. Psalm 2:7 sustains this doctrine. God the Father continues:

Ask of me, and I shall give thee the heathen for thine inheritance, and the uttermost parts of the earth for thy possession [Ps. 2:8].

The scepter of this universe will be held by a Man with nail-pierced hands. He is the One who is yet to rule.

This verse is often used in missionary conferences. I suppose I have heard a dozen sermons on missions using this verse of Scripture—and probably you have—but it ought never go to a missionary conference. It hasn't anything to do with missions. I remember listening to a graduate of Union Seminary in New York City bring a missionary message using this verse. I was then a student in seminary. As a student I did something that was very impolite, very rude. I think I've got more sense than to do it today. I went up to him after he had preached the message, and I asked, "Doctor, why didn't you use the next verse?" He acted as if he didn't hear me, although I am sure he did, and began talking with somebody there. I said to him the second time, "Doctor, why didn't you use the next verse?" This time he turned his back on me, and just ignored me. Well, I should have left, but I didn't. I walked around in front, and I said to him, "Doctor, why didn't you use the next verse?" He looked me right straight in the eye and said, "Because it would have ruined a missionary sermon." And it sure would have!

Notice the next verse, the verse that follows it:

Thou shalt break them with a rod of iron; thou shalt dash them in pieces like a potter's vessel [Ps. 2:9].

Do you think this is the Gospel of the grace of God we are to preach today? It is not. This passage hasn't any reference to Christ's first coming. This speaks of His second coming, when He comes to this earth to judge.

This is the way He will come the second time—to judge the earth. He has not asked me to apologize for Him, so I won't apologize. He says that He intends to come to this little planet and put down the rebellion that has broken out—and He will *break* them with the rod of iron. Maybe you don't like that. Well, you take it up with Him. He said it, and He is going to do it just that way.

Now I have a question to ask you, if you think He ought to do it the way some of our political leaders are suggesting. Suppose Jesus came back to this earth tomorrow, like He came some 2000 years ago, the man of Galilee, the carpenter of Nazareth, the gentle Jesus. Suppose He went to the Kremlin and knocked at the door. Whoever keeps the store over there would come and say, "Yes?" He would say, "I'm Jesus. I'm here to take over." Do you think they would say, "My, we have been waiting for you"? No, they'd put Him before a firing squad in the morning. My friend, how do you think He could take over if He came to Russia today? He would have to break them with a rod of iron, would He not? Apparently that is what He is going to do. Now suppose He goes to France. They don't want Him. Suppose He went down to Rome. I was there just a few weeks ago. I went over the Tiber and listened to a man speak. Although I could not understand what he was saying, I was told that he was telling the world how they ought to do it. He would like to take over. Suppose our Lord would go and knock on the door of the Vatican. The man with the long garment would come to the door, and the Lord Jesus would say, "I'm here to take over." What do you think he would say? I think he would say, "Now look, You've come a little too soon. I'm having trouble with some of my priests, but I'm going to work that out. I don't need You." I don't think he would want Him. Suppose He came to this country. Suppose He went to the Democratic headquarters, or the Republican headquarters, and said, "I'm here to take over." They would say, "We're getting ready for a presidential campaign, we've already got our candidates; we don't need You." Now maybe you think their reaction would be different. Maybe you are saying, "Oh, they would take Him." Then *why* don't they take Him? They will not because they won't have Him! Suppose He went to the World Council of Churches today, and He said to Protestantism, "I'm here." Would they receive Him? Then why don't they receive Him today? When He comes the second time He will come exactly as God said: "Thou shalt break them with a rod of iron; thou shalt dash them in pieces like a potter's vessel." He intends to put down the rebellion when He comes to this earth the next time. Oh, my friend, this namby-pamby way of thinking that our God is not going to judge! You and I are living in a world that is moving to judgment day, and God *is* going to judge.

CAMERA FOCUS: GOD THE HOLY SPIRIT

The camera in heaven goes off. The camera on earth comes on. Now God the Holy Spirit speaks:

> **Be wise now therefore, O ye kings: be instructed, ye judges of the earth.**
>
> **Serve the LORD with fear, and rejoice with trembling [Ps. 2:10–11].**

One of the most startling things I have encountered in studying the Bible the past few years is a little thing like this: God, in the history of this world, has always gotten a message to the rulers of this world. Always. No exception. Down yonder in the land of ancient Egypt, there was a Pharaoh on the throne, and there was boy Joseph in prison. God kept him in prison so that at the right moment He could bring him out to make him the prime minister of Pharaoh at one of the most crucial periods in the history of the world. That is the way God does it. Down yonder when the first great world power, Babylon, came into existence, God put the man Daniel at the side of Nebuchadnezzar. He not only became his prime minister, but also he brought him to a saving knowledge of the living God. And God kept him there until Cyrus, the Persian, came to the throne. And Cyrus even made his *decree* in the name of the living God. Napoleon said that he was a man of destiny, that he was told God had raised him up. It is interesting how God has gotten His Word to the rulers of this earth and to those who are in high places. God the Holy Spirit says to the rulers: "Serve the LORD with fear, and rejoice with trembling."

Also He says:

Kiss the Son, lest he be angry, and ye perish from the way, when his wrath is kindled but a little. Blessed are all they that put their trust in him [Ps. 2:12].

The late Dr. George Gill used to tell us in class, "'Kiss the Son' is the Old Testament way of saying, '. . . Believe on the Lord Jesus Christ, and thou shalt be saved . . .' (Acts 16:31)." "Kiss the Son."

Do you remember who kissed Him? Have you ever noted what our Lord said to Judas after he kissed Him? The theologians today argue about predestination and election and predetermination and foreknowledge, and that this man Judas could not help what he did since it had been prophesied he would do it. Now I'm going to let the theologians handle that. I'm just a poor preacher who doesn't know very much; so I stay away from those problems and let the theologians solve them. However, after I listen to them awhile I have a sneaking feeling they haven't solved them. Notice what the Bible says, and it is well to listen to the Bible rather than to the theologians. Remember at Jesus' betrayal when Judas led the mob out to apprehend Jesus in the

garden, he said, "I'll identify him for you by kissing Him." So he came
to Jesus and kissed Him. Have you noted what Jesus said to him?
"And Jesus said unto him, Friend, wherefore art thou come? . . ."
(Matt. 26:50). Why did He say that? Didn't He know why Judas had
kissed Him? Of course He did. Then why did He call him *friend*?
What did He mean? Let me suggest this. "Judas, you have just kissed
Me, which has fulfilled prophecy, and has satisfied all the theologians
who are going to come along. Now you are free to turn and accept Me,
free to turn that kiss of betrayal into a kiss of acceptance. You can do
that, Judas. You are a free moral agent." And the Spirit of God says,
"Kiss the Son. Believe on the Lord Jesus Christ, and thou shalt be
saved."

My friend, the Spirit of God today is in the world saying to mankind, "Kiss the Son before it is too late. Believe on the Lord Jesus
Christ before it is too late." He is coming some day, and He is going to
establish His kingdom here upon this earth. He is going to rule, and
He is going to put down all rebellion. He will bring peace and harmony to this little earth.

When I first went to Nashville, Tennessee, as a pastor, some
friends, thinking they were doing me a favor, called me and said, "We
have tickets for the symphony orchestra that's coming to town and we
want to take you as our guest." Well, I love music, but I know nothing
about it; and I can't sing it—I always help congregational singing by
keeping quiet. Frankly, I can't think of anything more boring than a
whole evening of symphony! But I had to go because they were polite
and I wanted to be polite, so I accepted graciously and went along. I
had never been to a thing like that before, and I was impressed by
what I saw. We went in, took our seats, and in a few moments the
musicians began to drift out from the stage sides. They were in shirt
sleeves for the most part, and each man went up to his instrument and
started tuning it. The fellows with the fiddles too big to put under
their chins sawed back and forth—oh, it sounded terrible. The fellows
with the little ones they put under their chins squeaked up and down
with those. The ones with the horns—oh my, nothing was in harmony.
It was a medley of discordant, confused noise. Then after they got
through with that kind of disturbance, they all disappeared again—

went out through the wings. Another five minutes went by, when all of a sudden the lights in the auditorium went off, the lights on the platform came on, and the musicians walked out. This time they had on their coats. My, they looked so nice. Each one came out and stood or sat at his instrument. Then there was a hush in the auditorium, a spotlight was focused on the wings, and the conductor stepped out. When he did, there was thunderous applause for him. He bowed. Then he came up to the podium and picked up a thin little stick. He turned around again to the audience and bowed, then turned his back to the audience, lifted that little stick—total silence came over that auditorium, you could have heard a pin drop—then he brought that little stick down. And, my friend, there were goose pimples all over me. I never heard such music in all my life. Oh, what harmony, what wonderful harmony there was!

Today I live in a world where every man is tooting his own little horn. Every little group wants to be heard. Everybody wants to tell you what he thinks. Everybody is playing his own little fiddle, and I want to tell you, it's a medley of discord. Everything is out of tune. But one of these days the spotlight is going on, and the Lord Jesus Christ will come. When He comes to this universe, He is going to lift His scepter, and everything that is out of tune with Him is going to be removed. Then when He comes down with that scepter—oh, the harmony that will be in this universe! I'm thankful today that I do live in a universe where I can bow to Him, and I can bring this little instrument of my body, my life, into tune with Him. I can bow to Him, and I can acknowledge Him, I can make Him my Savior and Lord.

PSALM 3

THEME: A morning prayer: the trials of the godly in Israel

Psalms 3—7 form a bridge, which I think of as a stairway between two messianic psalms. Psalm 2 is the prophetic rejection of God's anointed, and Psalm 8 is His ultimate victory as Man. The psalms between furnish the glue that holds these two messianic psalms together. They primarily describe the godly remnant of Israel during the time of the absence of the Messiah from the earth, especially during that time which our Lord labeled the Great Tribulation period. In these five psalms we have the record of Israel's trials, sorrows, confusions, problems, and sins. We also see their confidence in God, the promises of God, and their prayers for deliverance.

Trials and sorrows are shared by all godly people, regardless of who they are or in what period of history they live. The comfort given in these psalms is for all of God's children. There are three ways to look at these psalms. The *primary* interpretation, of course, concerns the personal experience of David. Then there is a direct *application* to the godly remnant in the nation of Israel during the Great Tribulation. There is also an application to God's people everywhere at any time in the history of the world. If we look at the psalms from this point of view, they will become more meaningful to us.

Psalm 3 is called "A Psalm of David when he fled from Absalom his son." (The historical record is in 2 Samuel, chapters 15—18.) This title tells us about the contents of this psalm. It tells us what went on in the heart of David when he had to flee from Jerusalem when Absalom his son rebelled against him. This psalm came out of the personal experience of David. He was in a difficult situation. He had become an outcast and a fugitive from his own city Jerusalem, which is called the city of David. He had been driven from the people he ruled. Absalom, his son, was in rebellion against him and seeking his life. Absalom's intention was actually to put his father to death. Your heart cannot help but go out to David during this heartbreaking experience.

As David fled, the enemy was on the sidelines cursing him. Abishai, one of his mighty men said, "Let me run a spear through him." David said, "Oh, no." The prophet Nathan had told David that God would punish him for his sins. In 2 Samuel 12:11 Nathan said to David, "Thus saith the LORD, Behold, I will raise up evil against thee out of thine own house, and I will take thy wives before thine eyes, and give them unto thy neighbour. . . ." Why would this happen? Because David had sinned greatly, and he was not going to get away with it. God has graciously forgiven David and restored him, but David has to reap the results of his sin; and it is in his son's rebellion that he does it. We find that David's enemies have increased on all sides and that the hearts of the men of Israel followed Absalom. The Scripture tells us, ". . . The hearts of the men of Israel are after Absalom" (2 Sam. 15:13). Absalom was an attractive young man. He was a clever politician who was able to promise the people many good things which he would not have been able to deliver.

During the time of Absalom's rebellion there were many others who rose up against David. He went out of Jerusalem barefoot and weeping. He passed over Kidron. It looked as if there was no help for him at all.

With this background in mind, let us look at Psalm 3.

LORD, how are they increased that trouble me! many are they that rise up against me [Ps. 3:1].

David is speaking right out of his heart, friend, as he leaves Jerusalem.

Many there be which say of my soul, There is no help for him in God. Selah [Ps. 3:2].

Many said that David would find no help from God, that God had forsaken him. But God did not forsake him. When someone says to me, "I cannot understand how God put up with a man like David," I always feel like saying, "Well, if God put up with David, maybe He will put up with you and me." Be thankful that we have this kind of a God, friend. He puts up with folk like David, and He will forgive any believer who comes to Him in repentance. This doesn't mean that David did not pay for his sin, because he did.

At the end of the second verse we find the word *Selah*. There has been a great deal of discussion as to the meaning of this word. It occurs about seventy-one times in the Psalms. I believe the Psalms were set to music, to be played by an orchestra and sung by great choirs. I am sure that Jerusalem became famous throughout the world, and people came from near and far to hear the music and the singing of these psalms. I think *selah* was probably a musical rest, a musical pause. For the common layman who does not understand much about music it means, "Stop, look, and listen." That is the type of sign you have at railroad crossings. I remember the days when my dad would drive a buggy into Snyder, Texas, and I would sometimes go with him. He would always stop at the railroad crossing. There wouldn't be a train within ten miles of the place, but we always stopped, looked, and listened. When we come to these marvelous psalms, we should stop, look, and listen. *Selah* reminds us to do that. That is what we should do when we come to the Word of God.

The word *selah* probably ends the first stanza of this psalm. Now David says:

> **I laid me down and slept; I awaked; for the LORD sustained me.**
>
> **I will not be afraid of ten thousands of people, that have set themselves against me round about [Ps. 3:5–6].**

This has been called "a morning psalm." This is a good psalm with which to start the day. In spite of all the problems and troubles that David had, he trusted in the Lord. He could sleep at night. He wasn't able to get an aspirin tablet or a sedative to put him to sleep. He simply trusted in the Lord, pillowed his head on the promises of God, and went to sleep.

"I awaked; for the LORD sustained me." Then David says that he would not be afraid if ten thousands of people set themselves against him. Even though the whole world was against him, David says he will not be afraid.

Cromwell is considered by many to be the bravest man who ever lived. Someone asked him, "What is the explanation of your bravery?" Cromwell replied, "Because I fear God, I have no man to fear." Martin Luther also took that position. If there were more fear of God today, there would be less of this licking of men's boots. There are some men who go around with their tongues black because they spend so much time licking the boots of men. Why do they do it? There is no fear of God in them. The thing that gives you courage is to fear God. If you fear God, then you have no man to fear. David trusted in God.

> **Arise, O LORD; save me, O my God: for thou hast smitten all mine enemies upon the cheek bone; thou hast broken the teeth of the ungodly [Ps. 3:7].**

It really hurts to get hit on the cheekbone. When you get hit there, it will really knock you out; and David had probably experienced that. He says that his enemies had been smitten on the cheekbone. God had also broken the teeth of the ungodly—they were not able to bite David anymore.

> **Salvation belongeth unto the LORD: thy blessing is upon thy people. Selah [Ps. 3:8].**

Salvation unto the Lord—*belongeth* is a word which was inserted by the translators. This is a great Scripture. The Lord is the author of salvation. David never thought of salvation as a coin that you could put in your pocket and lose. He never thought it was something he would have to work out. Salvation was the *gift* of God. "Salvation . . . unto the LORD: thy blessing is upon thy people."

Then comes the word *selah*. We are to stop, look, and listen. David has said some wonderful things about God in this psalm. For example, in verse 3 David calls Him his "shield." As a shield, God covers those who are His own. In Ephesians 6:16 we are told to take the shield of faith, as believers. David knew something about what the shield would do—he used it a great deal. God was also his "glory." That is, David believed in the presence of God. The cloud of glory, you remember, was spread over Israel. It was a visible sign of the presence of God in the midst of His people. Today we walk by faith, and the glory of God is with us, friend; He makes Himself real to those who are His own. God was also the "uplifter" of David's head. How could that be? God promised to build David a house and give him a blessing, a glory, and a kingdom. David said, "He is going to lift my head." We may be down, my friend, but He is going to lift us up. This is a marvelous psalm, is it not?

PSALM 4

THEME: *An evening prayer: the plea of the Son of man and those who plead in His name*

This brief psalm divides itself like this: a cry—verses 1–3; a correction—verses 4–5; a confidence—verses 6–8.

The psalm has a musical inscription "To the chief Musician on Neginoth, A Psalm of David." Apparently a neginoth is some sort of instrument; it is the belief of many that it is a stringed instrument. Probably this psalm was played as a solo on a neginoth.

The psalm begins with a great cry—the refuge of the people of God in the time of trouble is always prayer. And God is their shield, as we have seen.

> **Hear me when I call, O God of my righteousness: thou hast enlarged me when I was in distress; have mercy upon me, and hear my prayer [Ps. 4:1].**

Distress indicates pressure—the pressures of life are great. They are great in our day, and we need the encouragement that we find in the Word of God. "The LORD is nigh unto all them that call upon him, to all that call upon him in truth" (Ps. 145:18). Again in Psalm 50:15 we read, "And call upon me in the day of trouble: I will deliver thee, and thou shalt glorify me." In Isaiah 65:24 God tells us, "And it shall come to pass, that before they call, I will answer; and while they are yet speaking, I will hear." Psalm 18:6 is very personal: "In my distress I called upon the LORD, and cried unto my God: he heard my voice out of his temple, and my cry came before him, even into his ears." In Psalm 55:16 we are told, "As for me, I will call upon God; and the LORD shall save me." Psalm 86:7 says, "In the day of my trouble I will call upon thee: for thou wilt answer me." Finally, Psalm 91:15 says, "He shall call upon me, and I will answer him: I will be with him in trouble; I will deliver him, and honour him." The Bible is just filled with these wonderful promises. The cry of the psalmist in Psalm 4 is that God be with him.

> **O ye sons of men, how long will ye turn my glory into shame? how long will ye love vanity, and seek after leasing? Selah [Ps. 4:2].**

Leasing is falsehood.

> **But know that the Lord hath set apart him that is godly for himself: the Lord will hear when I call unto him [Ps. 4:3].**

How wonderful He is! God will hear our prayer.
   Then he gives two verses of correction, which is sort of a warning.

> **Stand in awe, and sin not: commune with your own heart upon your bed, and be still. Selah [Ps. 4:4].**

Stand in awe is better translated *tremble*, and do not sin. We don't see much trembling today.

> **Offer the sacrifices of righteousness, and put your trust in the Lord [Ps. 4:5].**

Paul expressed this thought to the Ephesian Christians: "Be ye angry, and sin not: let not the sun go down upon your wrath" (Eph. 4:26).
   Now notice his confidence and the assurance of faith.

> **There be many that say, Who will shew us any good? Lord, lift thou up the light of thy countenance upon us [Ps. 4:6].**

Many folk say, "Nothing is right anymore." How we need the Lord to lift up the light of His countenance upon us!

Thou hast put gladness in my heart, more than in the time that their corn and their wine increased [Ps. 4:7].

David was like the rest of us—his heart failed in the time of trouble. Around him were unbelievers, his own people, who were mocking him, "God is not going to do anything for him." But God *did* do something for him. "Thou hast put gladness in my heart, more than in the time that their corn and their wine increased." David found that God was good to him. And God is good to us, my friend.

Notice how this evening psalm concludes:

I will both lay me down in peace, and sleep: for thou, LORD, only makest me dwell in safety [Ps. 4:8].

My friend, do you need a sleeping pill at night? Have you ever tried Psalm 4? It is lots better than any brand of sleeping pill you have used.

Oh, how wonderful these psalms are for us today, and how much they will mean to God's people in that coming day of trouble.

PSALM 5

THEME: A morning prayer: a cry of the godly in the time of great trouble

Psalm 5 is included in the section which forms a stairway between two messianic psalms. This group of psalms (3—7) actually tells a story. They are, first of all, a picture of a personal experience of David. Secondly, they reveal prophetically the picture of the nation Israel during the Great Tribulation period. Also they have very real applications for us today, for they involve great principles. They have messages for God's people in all ages and in all times.

This is a psalm written by David, and it has as its inscription: "To the chief Musician upon Nehiloth." Psalm 4 was on neginoth, a stringed instrument, and this one, nehiloth, is generally believed to have been a wind instrument, a flute. David, the sweet psalmist of Israel, set most of these psalms to music. Possibly a choir also sang this psalm to the accompaniment of flutes. Arthur Pridham states the tone and general character of this psalm very nicely: "It is a prayer of faith, sent up from a heart in which the discernment of God as the shield and rewarder of them that seek Him, is found in union with a very deep sense of the prevailing evil and ungodliness which daily present themselves to the contemplation of the faithful. Vexing of soul because of the abundance of iniquity is thus a leading feature in its general expression." Pridham also makes this very interesting statement: "Hence patience is wrought in tribulation. Joy abounds in the sure hope of a deliverance, which is deferred only by the councils of unerring love." This pretty well sums up this very magnificent psalm.

It is called a morning psalm, and notice how it begins:

Give ear to my words, O LORD, consider my meditation.

Hearken unto the voice of my cry, my King, and my God: for unto thee will I pray.

My voice shalt thou hear in the morning, O LORD; in the morning will I direct my prayer unto thee, and will look up [Ps. 5:1–3].

Now let me give you a little different translation: "Give ear to my words, O Jehovah, give heed to my meditation. Listen to the voice of my cry, my King, and my God; for to thee do I pray. Jehovah, in the morning shalt thou hear my voice; in the morning will I come before thee, and expectantly look up." This psalm is a morning prayer—in the morning his voice would be lifted unto God. The morning is a mighty good time to lift your heart to God in prayer.

For thou art not a God that hath pleasure in wickedness: neither shall evil dwell with thee.

The foolish shall not stand in thy sight: thou hatest all workers of iniquity.

Thou shalt destroy them that speak leasing: the LORD will abhor the bloody and deceitful man.

But as for me, I will come into thy house in the multitude of thy mercy: and in thy fear will I worship toward thy holy temple [Ps. 5:4–7].

A little different translation at this point I think will be helpful for a better understanding of this passage. "For no God art thou whom wickedness can please. The evil man cannot dwell with thee. The arrogant shall not dare to stand before thine eyes. Thou hatest all workings of iniquity. Thou wilt destroy them that speak lies: the man of blood and deceit Jehovah abhorreth. As for me, through thy great mercy will I enter thy house. I will fall down, facing thy holy temple in fear."

This is the comfort of the godly. When you look about you today, you may have (as I do) a sinking feeling as you see the evil that is abroad and the iniquity that abounds. It is something that makes you sick at heart. What is the comfort of the godly in days like these? The psalmist tells us. The hatred that he has in his heart for evil reveals that he is on God's side. God also hates it. It also makes God sick to look down on this sinful world of today. Wickedness does not please God, nor will it please those who know God. Evil cannot dwell with Him, for ". . . God is light, and in him is no darkness at all" (1 John 1:5). Habakkuk said it like this (when the Lord told him that the Chaldeans were going to invade God's land): "Thou art of purer eyes than to behold evil, and canst not look on iniquity . . ." (Hab. 1:13). Wickedness may prosper for a time, but the day is surely coming which will bring destruction and eternal shame to those who practice lies and iniquity. God has made it very, very clear that there is a day of judgment coming, and evil is not going to prevail. God spells it out in Revelation 21:8 which says, "But the fearful, and unbelieving, and the abominable, and murderers, and whoremongers, and sorcerers, and idolaters, and all liars, shall have their part in the lake which burneth with fire and brimstone: which is the second death." Now I may sound like an antiquated preacher referring to a passage like this, but I believe that the judgment of God is coming upon this earth.

> **Lead me, O LORD, in thy righteousness because of mine enemies; make thy way straight before my face.**

> **For there is no faithfulness in their mouth; their inward part is very wickedness; their throat is an open sepulchre; they flatter with their tongue [Ps. 5:8-9].**

A different translation is: "Jehovah, lead me in thy righteousness because of my foes." He is saying, "My enemies are watching me. They want me to stumble and fall, but I want to glorify You." Therefore he is praying to God that He will not let him stumble and fall, and that He will lead him. He prays, "Make thy paths straight before me, for in their mouth is nothing trustworthy; they are inwardly full of depravity; their throat is an open sepulchre." By the way, this is quoted in Romans 3:13 by the apostle Paul. "They make their tongues smooth"—they are glib of tongue. They don't seem to know what the truth is, and they seldom tell it.

Destroy thou them, O God; let them fall by their own counsels; cast them out in the multitude of their transgressions; for they have rebelled against thee.

But let all those that put their trust in thee rejoice: let them ever shout for joy, because thou defendest them: let them also that love thy name be joyful in thee.

For thou, LORD, wilt bless the righteous; with favour wilt thou compass him as with a shield [Ps. 5:10–12].

Or to translate it another way: "Destroy them, O God, let them fall by their own counsels; cast them out in the multitude of their transgressions, for they have rebelled against Thee. And all who seek refuge with Thee shall rejoice; forever shall they shout for joy because of thy protection, and they shall exult in Thee and love Thy name, for Thou, Jehovah, will bless the righteous: with favour wilt Thou surround him as with a shield." Prayer is this man's resource and recourse when he looks at the wickedness all about him. He prays for that guidance which will enable him to walk in a way that will not bring disrepute upon the name of God.

In verse 10 the psalmist asks the Lord to destroy the enemy. This is the first imprecatory prayer recorded in the Psalms. Later on I will have time to develop that subject. There are certain prayers that David prayed where he asked God for justice; he asked God to intervene and bring judgment. Some of them are very harsh. Isaiah prayed that way in Isaiah 64:1–2, when he said, "Oh that thou wouldest rend the heavens, that thou wouldest come down, that the mountains might flow down at thy presence, As when the melting fire burneth, the fire causeth the waters to boil, to make thy name known to thine adversaries, that the nations may tremble at thy presence!" Judgment must fall some day upon the transgressors. Scripture makes it very clear that God will take vengeance.

The Lord, you remember, told the parable concerning the widow who took her case to an earthly judge, saying, ". . . Avenge me of mine adversary. And he would not for a while: but afterward he said within himself, Though I fear not God, nor regard man; Yet because this widow troubleth me, I will avenge her, lest by her continual coming she weary me. And the Lord said, Hear what the unjust judge saith. And shall not God avenge his own elect, which cry day and night unto him, though he bear long with them? I tell you that he will avenge them speedily . . ." (Luke 18:3–8). And David in his day prayed for vengeance.

For a Christian to pray these prayers during these days I think is absolutely sinful. You say, "You don't mean that!" I certainly do mean it. This is where I think a proper interpretation of Scripture is essential. There are many people who want to get rid of this portion of the Word of God. There are even people who say this is not even God's Word because it is no expression for a Christian today. Well, who said it was? This is going to be for God's people during the Great Tribulation. In that day these people under law will pray this kind of prayer as they did in the past under law. And God intends to hear His people, and He intends to bring vengeance upon their enemies. We are to do things differently during this age. Matthew 5:44 says, "But I say unto you, Love your enemies, bless them that curse you, do good to them that hate you, and pray for them which despitefully use you, and persecute you." This is difficult to do, I will grant you that, but that is what the Lord asks us to do. In Romans 12:19 we are told, "Dearly beloved, avenge not yourselves, but rather give place unto wrath: for it is written, Vengeance is mine; I will repay, saith the Lord." God says that He will take care of any reprisals. When we get hit in the nose, it is human nature to want to hit back. But when we take matters into our own hands, we are not walking with Him by faith. God wants us to trust Him to take care of our enemies.

When the Lord Jesus Christ was here on earth and was so brutally treated, He did not strike back. He wants those who are His own in the church today to take that same position. But God has said, "Vengeance is mine; I will repay." God intends to take care of it some day.

This is a marvelous psalm. What a comfort it will be to God's people in the time of severe persecution!

PSALM 6

THEME: A cry for mercy

The man in this psalm has looked all about him and has seen the wickedness on every hand. He has also looked in his own heart and recognized that he is not perfect before God at all. If the previous psalms and prayers had to do with morning and evening, this psalm has to do with the darkest night. This psalm is addressed to "The chief Musician on Neginoth upon Sheminith." We are introduced to a new term *sheminith*. It means "upon the octave," and there are those who believe it should be sung by male voices. Psalm 5 is an imprecatory psalm, and Psalm 6 is a penitential psalm, a cry of repentance, and plea for mercy.

> **O Lord, rebuke me not in thine anger, neither chasten me in thy hot displeasure.**
>
> **Have mercy upon me, O Lord; for I am weak: O Lord, heal me; for my bones are vexed.**
>
> **My soul is also sore vexed: but thou, O Lord, how long?**
>
> **Return, O Lord, deliver my soul: oh save me for thy mercies' sake [Ps. 6:1–4].**

The psalmist sees his own need. When he does, there is a wonderful cry of repentance. Next we have his confession.

> **For in death there is no remembrance of thee: in the grave who shall give thee thanks?**
>
> **I am weary with my groaning; all the night make I my bed to swim; I water my couch with my tears.**
>
> **Mine eye is consumed because of grief; it waxeth old because of all mine enemies [Ps. 6:5–7].**

I think we have here a picture of David, and I think we have a picture of the Lord Jesus Christ. I think it is also a picture of Israel in the last days, and a picture of believers right now—you and me. What a psalm this is! This is a cry for mercy out of the very depths of despair. Only mercy can save us. We are told over and over again in the New Testament that God is rich in mercy. He has had to use a lot of His mercy on me, but He has some left over for you. He has plenty of mercy, and we certainly need it.

Isaiah 52:14 says of the Lord Jesus, ". . . his visage was so marred more than any man, and his form more than the sons of men." In Psalm 69:3 the Lord says, "I am weary of my crying: my throat is dried: mine eyes fail while I wait for my God." Again in Psalm 42:3 the Lord says, "My tears have been my meat day and night, while they continually say unto me, Where is thy God?" In Psalm 38:10 He says, "My heart panteth, my strength faileth me: as for the light of mine eyes, it also is gone from me." Finally, in Psalm 88:9 the Lord says, "Mine eye mourneth by reason of affliction: LORD, I have called daily upon thee, I have stretched out my hands unto thee." In all of these expressions, and I have given you only a very small segment, the Spirit of Christ speaks prophetically of His own suffering through which He would pass in the days of His humiliation.

His people, the nation Israel, that remnant in the Great Tribulation, will also pass through suffering. Today many of God's saints are passing through it. The great comfort is that He has been through it. These are the things that He has suffered, that He endured. Regardless of what you are going through today, He has already been through it, and He can comfort you. How wonderful it is to have a Savior like the Lord Jesus Christ.

> **Depart from me, all ye workers of iniquity; for the LORD hath heard the voice of my weeping [Ps. 6:8].**

Here is the answer to prayer:

> **The LORD hath heard my supplication; the LORD will receive my prayer [Ps. 6:9].**

In Hebrews 5:7 we are told concerning the Lord Jesus, "Who in the days of his flesh, when he had offered up prayers and supplications with strong crying and tears unto him that was able to save him from death, and was heard in that he feared." That is our confidence today. God will hear and answer our prayer when we are in deep trouble. Isn't that a comfort to you, friend? You may be in a very hard place right at the moment. If you are, this psalm is for you.

PSALM 7

THEME: A cry for revenge

S omeone has suggested that over this psalm should be written: "Shall not the Judge of all the earth do right?" (Gen. 18:25).

Notice that the inscription is "Shiggaion of David, which he sang unto the LORD, concerning the words of Cush the Benjamite." Although we cannot be dogmatic on the meaning of *shiggaion*, it is thought that it means "crying aloud." This is David crying aloud in song. How I would love to have heard him sing this psalm. This psalm is a *loud* cry. I think it reveals prophetically the persecution and the final suffering of the God-fearing remnant of Israel during the time of the Great Tribulation. It is the outcry against the "man of sin," a theme that is carried into the next psalm. Notice David's confidence in prayer:

> O LORD my God, in thee do I put my trust: save me from all them that persecute me, and deliver me:
>
> Lest he tear my soul like a lion, rending it in pieces, while there is none to deliver [Ps. 7:1–2].

Arno Gaebelein's translation reads: "Jehovah, my God, in thee I seek shelter. Save me from my pursuers, and rescue me, lest like a lion he tear my soul rending in pieces, and no one to deliver" (*The Book of Psalms*, p. 40). Who is that lion? That is Satan, whom Peter says is on the prowl. "Be sober, be vigilant; because your adversary the devil, as a roaring lion, walketh about, seeking whom he may devour" (1 Pet. 5:8).

Then he speaks of unjust persecution:

> O LORD my God, if I have done this; if there be iniquity in my hands;

If I have rewarded evil unto him that was at peace with me; (yea, I have delivered him that without cause is mine enemy:) [Ps. 7:3–4].

Unjust and innocent suffering in this world is something I don't understand. I don't propose to understand it, but I want to say this to you: I know Somebody who does understand it, and He is going to explain it to us one day. There are things in my life and things in your life that we don't understand. I can't explain your trouble, because I don't even know why I have had to go through certain things; but He is going to explain it someday.

Now we come to the wonderful part. This is not the darkness of night as we saw in Psalm 6, but this is morning light.

Arise, O LORD, in thine anger, lift up thyself because of the rage of mine enemies: and awake for me to the judgment that thou hast commanded [Ps. 7:6].

He cries for God to avenge and vindicate him.

God judgeth the righteous, and God is angry with the wicked every day [Ps. 7:11].

At the time I am writing this, we are in a time of the "new morality," which is really just old immorality. God doesn't go along with it; He is not changing His standards to conform to modern thought. Because of this, we can sing with David:

I will praise the LORD according to his righteousness: and will sing praise to the name of the LORD most high [Ps. 7:17].

My friend, God will deal with sin and wickedness, and He will finally eradicate it from His universe. Praise the Lord!

PSALM 8

THEME: A messianic psalm emphasizing the humanity of Christ and His ultimate victory as Man

Messianic psalms are so called because they are quoted in the New Testament in direct reference to the Lord Jesus Christ. Psalm 8 is quoted three times in the New Testament. In fact, the Lord Jesus Himself quoted from this psalm. In Matthew 21 we have recorded what is called the triumphal entry of Christ into Jerusalem. The children in the temple were saying, ". . . Hosanna to the son of David" (Matt. 21:9). The chief priests and the scribes said, "Do you hear what they are saying?" It was at this time that Jesus said, ". . . Yea; have ye never read, Out of the mouth of babes and sucklings thou hast perfected praise?" (Matt. 21:16). Our Lord was quoting Psalm 8:2. He was telling the chief priests and the scribes that it would be a good idea if they read this Scripture so that they would understand why the children were saying this.

The second quotation from this psalm is found in 1 Corinthians 15:27, the resurrection chapter: "For he hath put all things under his feet" (v. 6). It is quite obvious that this psalm does not refer to our day, as Paul explains: "For he hath put all things under his feet. But when he saith all things are put under him, it is manifest that he is excepted, which did put all things under him."

We today do not see all things put under Him, that is for sure. However, the most complete quotation is found in Hebrews 2:5–8, which makes it very clear that Psalm 8 refers to our Lord Jesus Christ: "For unto the angels hath he not put in subjection the world to come, whereof we speak. But one in a certain place testified, saying, What is man, that thou art mindful of him? or the son of man, that thou visitest him? Thou madest him a little lower than the angels; thou crownedst him with glory and honour, and didst set him over the works of thy hands: Thou hast put all things in subjection under his feet. For in that he put all in subjection under him, he left nothing that is not put under him. But now we see not yet all things put under him." Again it is called to our attention that you and I live in a day when all things are not put under Him. Obviously Psalm 8 looks to the future.

Read Hebrews 2:9: "But we see Jesus, who was made a little lower than the angels for the suffering of death, crowned with glory and honour; that he by the grace of God should taste death for every man." Psalm 8 is talking about Jesus.

Now this second great messianic psalm begins with the statement: "O LORD our Lord, how excellent is thy name in all the earth!" And the psalm closes with "O LORD our Lord, how excellent is thy name in all the earth!"

This is not a reference to the present hour in which we are living. God's name is not very excellent in the world today. Not long ago on the golf course I heard an old man, who was standing right on the threshold of eternity, use the name of the Lord in vain in a way that was absolutely uncalled for. Walking down the street I heard a very nicely dressed, refined looking, gentle-woman, who looked like a grandmother, swear. My, how she could swear! God's name is not very excellent today. The fact of the matter is that people today are not saying very much about God. I notice on the newscasts that God is never mentioned. He makes the news, too, but He is never brought into the picture. God is recognized in insurance policies that insure houses that are destroyed by fire or by an "act of God"! Do they think the Lord is running around destroying houses? That is the only publicity God gets today. It is all bad as far as He is concerned. He is being left out and left out purposely. His Word is not wanted in the schools. These broad-minded liberals, who believe that everybody should be heard, think pornography should be permitted because the liberties of people should not be curtailed. Well, friend, don't I have a share in that liberty? I would like to have prayer in schools for my grandchildren. How about you? I would like some public recognition of God. I would like to have prayer in public places. Have I no liberties any longer in this land of ours? No, God's name is not excellent today.

The other night I watched a thrilling travelogue on television. Some men climbed to the top of Mount Everest, and the wind at the top was terrific. That old mountain was really talking back to them, letting them know that man is nothing. But there was no mention of God. Mountains are just a bunch of dirt, rocks, and a few trees; they do not talk or become violent or make men feel little. It is the God who made the mountain who does that. It was God on top of Mount Everest who let those men know how really insignificant they were. But the men did not learn how great God is; they just talked about nature. May I say to you that God's name is not excellent in the world today. Not at all.

This first verse in Psalm 8 is a prophecy. It looks to the future, a glorious future. It is a messianic psalm in which we see God's Man. It emphasizes the humanity of Christ and His ultimate victory as Man. In Psalm 2 we saw man in rejection and man's rebellion against God. In Psalm 8 we see that man finally gains control of this earth, and the day will come when God's name will be excellent in all the earth.

At this point I should mention that this psalm is addressed to "the chief Musician upon Gittith." Both Psalm 81 and Psalm 84 are also dedicated to "The chief Musician upon Gittith." What does that mean? The "gittith" has generally been interpreted as a musical instrument, a type of lyre. A Jewish scholar said that the word *gittith* was taken from the name Gath, and it was an instrument known in Gath. You will recall that David found shelter in Gath when he was escaping from King Saul. He probably learned to play this strange instrument at that time, and later introduced it to Israel. The Vulgate and the Septuagint translate the word *gittith* as "winepress." I think there is significance in that also, as Psalm 8 reveals the winepress of suffering that the Lord Jesus went into for you and me. As Man He tasted death for all men; He tasted the *bitterness* of the winepress. Later on, Isaiah will tell us that the Lord Jesus is coming from Edom. He says: "I have trodden the winepress alone; and of the people there was none with me: for I will tread them in mine anger, and trample them in my fury; and their blood shall be sprinkled upon my garments, and I will stain all my raiment" (Isa. 63:3). The juice of the grapes on His garments is not His own blood but that of His enemies.

You see, if the blood of Christ means nothing to you now and you are not saved, you will have to be judged. It is either His blood, or yours, my friend. That is the position of man in the world today.

Psalm 8 is a psalm of David. There are those who try to read into it "the death for the son," supposing that David wrote it at the time of the death of Bathsheba's infant son or on the occasion of the death of the giant Goliath. I mention all of these theories because this is a psalm that apparently has a great and deep meaning. I had a professor once who gave this psalm the title: "Stars and Sucklings." This psalm goes all the way from the heavens—the moon and the stars—to nursing children. Also this psalm goes along with Psalm 19, another nature psalm, which speaks of the Scriptures and the sun. But the sun is not mentioned here in Psalm 8 at all.

> **O LORD our Lord, how excellent is thy name in all the earth! who hast set thy glory above the heavens.**
>
> **Out of the mouth of babes and sucklings hast thou ordained strength because of thine enemies, that thou mightest still the enemy and the avenger [Ps. 8:1–2].**

The Lord made the truth of this verse clear when He said on earth, ". . . Verily I say unto you, Except ye be converted, and become as little children, ye shall not enter into the kingdom of heaven" (Matt. 18:3). It was children who cried, ". . . Hosanna to the son of David . . ." (Matt. 21:15) during His so-called triumphal entry into Jerusalem. Actually I do not consider it a triumphal entry. We must wait until He comes to earth again; then He will have a *real* triumphal entry. This is just a little picture of the fact that He is coming to earth again; and, when He does, He will establish His kingdom. In the meantime we must be converted and become as little children. I think this means that you and I must be born again and become little children. Like little children, we put aside all of our boasting and come in simple faith. How tremendous is the faith of a little child.

In this psalm we see the Lord as Creator. You have nature, the creation, and you have man, the creature. You have a relationship here.

**When I consider thy heavens, the work of thy fingers,
the moon and the stars, which thou hast ordained [Ps.
8:3].**

"Which thou hast ordained" means that God put them in their places.
In Southern California I often look at the moon and a star that is very
bright when it gets over into the southwest—which means it is located
out yonder over the South Pacific. I have often wondered why it is
there. I know only that it is there because Jesus wants it to be there.
He put it there. In my study I have certain things placed here and
there. I have a book in a certain place—because that is where I want
it. Now the stars are not arranged according to the way I want them—
I might move that one out in the southwest—but they are placed
where our Lord Jesus wants them to be. He is the One who is ordain-
ing.

The heavens are the work of His fingers. It is interesting that when
the Word speaks of salvation, it refers to the bared *arm* of the Lord:
"Who hath believed our report? and to whom is the arm of the LORD
revealed?" (Isa. 53:1). But when it speaks of the creation of the heavens and the earth, it calls it His *finger-work*. As John Wesley put it,
"God created the heavens and the earth and didn't half try." Creation
was His finger-work, like the crocheting of a woman.

God put His glory above His creation. It is great to us, and there is a
glory in creation, but we don't worship His creation. We worship the
Creator. His finger-work tells out His glory and His power.

**What is man, that thou art mindful of him? and the son
of man, that thou visitest him? [Ps. 8:4].**

There are those still working on the problem of, "What is man?" Man
is a complicated creature. He is a human being. He belongs to the
human race, and there are people still trying to figure out how he got
here. The Bible says that God created us and put us on earth. Then
man went afoul, he turned aside, he disbelieved God, and he dis-
obeyed Him. Why would God be mindful of man? Why didn't God
just wipe man out and get rid of him?

Man is a great failure. We don't like to hear that. We want to hear about success. Sometimes I think the most difficult job in the world is to be a cancer specialist. Since I have had cancer, I have gotten pretty close to that group, and they are pessimists, as I see it. They don't have many success stories in their field. Well, man doesn't have a success story; he is really a miserable failure. He has gotten his world in a mess. The psalmist asks, "What is man, that thou art mindful of him?" I will tell you why man is important. About two thousand years ago the Lord Jesus Christ visited him. He made a trip to earth and died on a cross to let us know that He loved us. He did not save us by love; He saved us by grace because we did not have anything to offer—we were not worth saving. Yet God the Son came to this earth. I don't know if there are any other planets which are inhabited—there may be—but I know that Christ has not been there to die on a cross. He came only here for that purpose.

> **For thou hast made him a little lower than the angels,
> and hast crowned him with glory and honour [Ps. 8:5].**

When the Lord Jesus made Old Testament appearances, He came as *the* Angel of the Lord; but when He came to Bethlehem, He came much lower than that—He came to the level of man.

> **Thou madest him to have dominion over the works of thy
> hands; thou hast put all things under his feet [Ps. 8:6].**

Man was given dominion over the works of God's hands, but man lost that. Man does not control this universe today. Science thought it had things under control, but now we find that science has polluted this earth; and it looks as if our earth will become a big garbage can. Science is responsible for polluting this earth. If you have been worshiping science and want to get out of the garbage can, you need a God who can help you.

"Thou madest him to have dominion . . . thou hast put all things under his feet"—but they haven't been put there yet, and won't be until Jesus returns.

All sheep and oxen, yea, and the beasts of the field;

The fowl of the air, and the fish of the sea, and whatsoever passeth through the paths of the seas [Ps. 8:7–8].

God made it all. He is the Creator. God made the beasts of the field, the fowl of the air, and the fish of the sea. God made it all. He is the Creator. He made you and me. In Romans 1:20 Paul says, "For the invisible things of him from the creation of the world are clearly seen, being understood by the things that are made, even his eternal power and Godhead; so that they are without excuse." We can see God's handiwork by simply looking around.

O LORD our Lord, how excellent is thy name in all the earth! [Ps. 8:9].

Not today, but someday the name of the Lord will be excellent in all the earth. In our time, we live in a universe that is groaning, travailing in pain, waiting for the redemption (Rom. 8:22). But God is above all creation. He has set His glory above the heavens. And up yonder is that Man who two thousand years ago came down to this earth to be born in Bethlehem. He is seated now in glory at God's right hand. Only by faith will we be able to see Him.

"But we all, with open face beholding as in a glass the glory of the Lord, are changed into the same image from glory to glory, even as by the Spirit of the Lord" (2 Cor. 3:18). "Beloved, now are we the sons of God, and it doth not yet appear what we shall be: but we know that, when he shall appear, we shall be like him; for we shall see him as he is" (1 John 3:2). What a glorious prospect this is for the child of God!

Once again I would like to remind you that this is a messianic psalm. It emphasizes the humanity of Christ and His ultimate victory as Man. We have just stood on the fringe of this glorious psalm, friend, that sings praises to our Savior.

PSALMS 9 AND 10

THEME: Satan's man

We were climbing an ascending stairway between the first two messianic psalms (2 and 8). Psalm 8 was the pinnacle, and now we are starting down the mountain on the other side. The descent will be through seven psalms that tell out a prophetic story. We will get glimpses of the suffering of the Jewish remnant at the end time and also a glimpse of the "man of sin," also called "the lawless one," who is yet to appear upon the earth.

Psalm 9 and Psalm 10 are very closely connected. There is a certain alphabetical structure, an acrostic, that is not seen in our translation, but which can be seen in the original. As a result, you will find that the Septuagint and the Vulgate put these two psalms together and consider them as one. This psalm is addressed to "the chief Musician upon Muth-labben." What does this word mean? It means "death for the son," a subject that some authors identify with Psalm 8 as we have seen. I think it is generally accepted to be the inscription for Psalm 9. This psalm is ascribed to David, the sweet singer of Israel. There are those who see the death of Goliath in this psalm. Others identify it with the death of Bathsheba's son. It means "death of the son, the firstborn"; and I rather think that it refers to what happened in the land of Egypt when Israel was delivered from slavery through the death of the firstborn of Egypt.

It begins with a note of praise.

> **I will praise thee, O Lord, with my whole heart; I will shew forth all thy marvellous works.**
>
> **I will be glad and rejoice in thee: I will sing praise to thy name, O thou most High [Ps. 9:1–2].**

This psalm begins with praise just as Psalm 7 begins with praise. As in the seventh psalm, so in Psalm 9 the praise is in anticipation of the coming victory so beautifully predicted in Psalm 8, when all things will be put under the feet of Him who was made a little lower than the angels. In fact, the first section of this psalm is a prophetic forecast of what earthly conditions will be when the Son of Man has received the throne in righteousness and in peace. In view of the future deliverance, we have this great song of praise in which all earthly people will join in that day. We have a picture of this in the Book of Revelation when that great company out of the nation Israel, the church, and the twenty-four elders will share in a time of great praise unto God.

> **When mine enemies are turned back, they shall fall and perish at thy presence.**
>
> **For thou hast maintained my right and my cause; thou satest in the throne judging right [Ps. 9:3–4].**

Once again we move into the time of the kingdom that is mentioned in Psalm 8, when all things will be put under His feet. John Knox put it like this: "One with God is a majority." He was not so much concerned about having God on his side as he was making sure he was on God's side. The important thing to David was that his cause was right. Let's make sure, my friend, that we are on God's side.

Now he speaks of the coming judgment.

> **Thou hast rebuked the heathen, thou hast destroyed the wicked, thou hast put out their name for ever and ever [Ps. 9:5].**

"Thou hast rebuked the heathen" is better translated, "Thou hast rebuked the nations." What a psalm this is!

> **O thou enemy, destructions are come to a perpetual end: and thou hast destroyed cities; their memorial is perished with them [Ps. 9:6].**

This is a strong declaration of the judgment that is coming.

The question arises, Is there enough preaching today about judgment? I would say that there is enough preaching of a certain kind of judgment, but there are very few sermons on the subject of hell. Lately I have had the opportunity to hear more sermons than I have heard for years, and I notice two things about them. Most sermons are designed to comfort God's people. In fact, many sermons are geared for those who seem to have some sort of a complex or are just looking for a shoulder to cry on. However, a sermon I heard the other day was on the subject of hell; but the bitterness of the preacher came through. I feel that before a man preaches on hell he ought to search his own heart to make sure that the subject affects him—that his heart is broken because men are lost. An unbeliever made the following statement about Dwight L. Moody when he was told that Moody preached a sermon on hell: "I don't like to hear sermons on hell, but if there is any man who can preach on that subject, it is Dwight L. Moody." May I say to you, not only should there be sermons on hell, but the right kind of men should preach them. I suppose one of the reasons I don't preach more sermons on hell is because I think I should be deeply moved in my heart when I do talk about this subject.

The psalmist makes it clear that all the enemies of Israel are to be conquered. This is God's victory for the remnant that will be on His side. I think what we have here is the death of the son, the firstborn, in Egypt. This takes us right down to the place where anti-Semitism was born—it started in the land of Egypt. A new king in that land enslaved God's chosen people, and he tried to exterminate the whole race which would frustrate the grace and purpose of God in redemption. Ever since that time the nations have been Israel's enemies. They will continue to hate Israel until the day of deliverance comes. At this present moment there is a feeling of hatred toward the Jews.

In this next passage the kingdom and the throne of righteousness is established.

> **But the Lord shall endure for ever: he hath prepared his throne for judgment.**
>
> **And he shall judge the world in righteousness, he shall minister judgment to the people in uprightness [Ps. 9:7–8].**

"He shall judge the world in righteousness"—that is important. It is my feeling today that we are short on judges who will follow the law and assess a penalty when a penalty should be assessed. We have too many judges who are softhearted, and I sometimes think softheaded, who are trying to be popular. Righteousness is what is needed today. The One who makes the right is God. Right is not necessarily what you think or what I think. It was God who divided the light from the darkness. I have never been able to separate them. I have never gotten up before daylight, waved a wand, and brought up the sun. God does that. He is the One who declares what is right. If you don't think so, you are wrong. That is just the way it is. It is as simple as that. Someone has to make the rules. God makes the rules for this universe, and He is running it. God is going to be around for a long time, and I think He has that prerogative.

Now, moving down a few verses, we have a picture of the condition before Christ comes to establish His kingdom.

> **Have mercy upon me, O Lord; consider my trouble which I suffer of them that hate me, thou that liftest me up from the gates of death [Ps. 9:13].**

"Have mercy upon me, O Lord"—I don't know about you, but I need mercy from God. You may question that since I said there will be justice when He comes. But, you see, justice has already been established in the person of the Lord Jesus Christ when He bore our sins, and He has been made unto us righteousness. What I need today is mercy, and mercy is extended to us in the person of Jesus Christ.

> **That I may shew forth all thy praise in the gates of the daughter of Zion: I will rejoice in thy salvation [Ps. 9:14].**

And we need more folk to *rejoice* in God.

> **The heathen are sunk down in the pit that they made: in the net which they hid is their own foot taken [Ps. 9:15].**

The *heathen* is better translated "nations"—"The nations are sunk down in the pit that they made."

Look at the nations of the world today. Even the great nations of the world, including our own nation, have sunk down into a pit. We seem to be caught. This is the condition of the world at the present hour.

> **The LORD is known by the judgment which he executeth: the wicked is snared in the work of his own hands. Higgaion. Selah [Ps. 9:16].**

This is a tremendous verse!

> **The wicked shall be turned into hell, and all the nations that forget God [Ps. 9:17].**

A cry goes out: "The wicked shall be turned into hell [Sheol, that is, unto *death*], and all the nations that forget God." This is a great principle that God has put down.

> **For the needy shall not always be forgotten: the expectation of the poor shall not perish for ever [Ps. 9:18].**

"The needy shall not alway be forgotten"—they are today. Oh, there are poverty programs, but the man at the top always seems to get it before it reaches the poor. The poor will receive justice when the Lord Jesus comes. You know, we poor people ought to be more interested in the Lord. There are so many people in poverty who are turning to political parties and certain political candidates for help. Unfortunately, they are not going to receive much help. What the candidates are trying to do is to get into office. The Lord Jesus is not running for office—He is King of kings and Lord of lords. He is not anxious to please any party or any group on this earth. When Christ came to earth the first time, He came to do God's will. Since He is God, when He comes again He is going to do His own will. My friend, "the needy shall not always be forgotten: the expectation of the poor shall not perish for ever." They are expecting a great deal from man, but only God will meet their need.

> **Arise, O LORD; let not man prevail: let the heathen be judged in thy sight [Ps. 9:19].**

"Let the *nations* be judged"—the nations are yet to be judged, according to our Lord (Matt. 25:31–46), ". . . and he shall separate them one from another, as a shepherd divideth his sheep from the goats" (Matt. 25:32).

> **Put them in fear, O LORD: that the nations may know themselves to be but men. Selah [Ps. 9:20].**

There are some today who feel that they are operating in the position of God. Remember that the inscription of this psalm is "Muthlabben," meaning death for the son. If you consider the son to be Goliath or Pharaoh, both of them are little pictures of the Antichrist who is yet to come. He will be Satan's man, and he will put himself in the position of God. God will ultimately put him down.

Now when we come to Psalm 10, we still see Satan's man, the man of the earth, which closely identifies Psalm 10 with Psalm 9.

Notice how the wicked one is described:

> **Why standest thou afar off, O LORD? why hidest thou thyself in times of trouble?**
>
> **The wicked in his pride doth persecute the poor: let them be taken in the devices that they have imagined.**
>
> **For the wicked boasteth of his heart's desire, and blesseth the covetous, whom the LORD abhorreth [Ps. 10:1–3].**

There are two things that characterize the wicked in these verses: pride and boasting. Do you want to know who the wicked are as you look around the world? They are those who are filled with pride, the "great" of the earth, who have no place for God in their lives. Also they do a great deal of boasting. I don't know how you feel, but I am not impressed by politicians and world leaders who are always boasting that they will solve the problems of the world. They remind me of what Aesop said about a mountain that travailed and brought forth a mouse! They boast of doing great things, but they accomplish practically nothing. What a picture we have here of the wicked and the "wicked one," the Antichrist, who will be the false messiah. He is identified in this psalm. Pride identifies him.

> **The wicked, through the pride of his countenance, will not seek after God: God is not in all his thoughts [Ps. 10:4].**

"God is not in all his thoughts" is better translated: "All his thoughts are: there is no God." Antichrist will be an atheist.

In the time of David there began to emerge for the first time in history those who were atheists. There were no atheists at the beginning because they were too close to the mooring mast of revelation. After all, Noah knew a man who knew Adam. When you are that close to the time of creation, you are not apt to deny the existence of God. When the Ten Commandments were given, there was no commandment against atheism; but there was one against polytheism—the worship of many gods. The first commandment is: "Thou shalt have no other gods before me." The second commandment is: "Thou shalt not make unto thee any graven image, or any likeness of any thing that is in heaven above, or that is in the earth beneath, or that is in the water under the earth" (Exod. 20:3–4). There are two commandments against polytheism, and none against atheism because there were no atheists. However, David will mention atheism several times.

The Antichrist at the end times will be characterized by atheism, filled with pride and boasting.

> **His ways are always grievous; thy judgments are far above out of his sight: as for all his enemies, he puffeth at them.**

> **He hath said in his heart, I shall not be moved: for I shall
> never be in adversity [Ps. 10:5–6].**

This also characterizes man in our day—boasting of his prosperity and self-sufficiency. He feels no need of God.

Now notice something else that will characterize Antichrist:

> **Wherefore doth the wicked contemn God? he hath said
> in his heart, Thou wilt not require it [Ps. 10:13].**

Not only does he not believe in God, but he despises Him. It is inconsistent to despise Someone who does not exist; apparently He has to exist to build up this kind of bitterness and hatred.

When he says, "Thou wilt not require it," he is saying that there is no judgment. There is a great multitude of people emerging in our contemporary culture who are saying there is no God, or, if He exists, He is too far away for them to bother with; and they are confident there will be no judgment. My friend, if you take that position, anything goes. It is that philosophy that is behind the movement to abolish capital punishment or any kind of punishment or any kind of imprisonment for a criminal. The argument I hear is that methods used today do not *reform* criminals. Whoever said that the purpose of punishment and prisons was to *reform*? It never was intended to reform; it was intended to *deter* crime. God gave these laws to protect the innocent. And God's judgment is inevitable upon the earth. The closer we get to it, the less man believes it is coming.

God is probably the most unpopular Person in the world right now. Why? Because the wicked are in the saddle. We are moving toward the time when the sin of man will lead to the "man of sin," this final Antichrist.

> **The LORD is King for ever and ever: the heathen are per-
> ished out of his land.**
>
> **LORD, thou hast heard the desire of the humble: thou
> wilt prepare their heart, thou wilt cause thine ear to
> hear:**

To judge the fatherless and the oppressed, that the man of the earth may no more oppress [Ps. 10:16–18].

"The man of the earth" is Antichrist.

These are remarkable psalms, my friend, because they amplify a great many truths which we get historically and prophetically in other portions of the Word of God.

PSALM 11

THEME: *Testing of the righteous*

This is a wonderful little psalm of David, ascribed to the chief Musician. We are not told under what circumstances it was written, but obviously it came out of the persecution and trials in the life of David. I am going to give an extended quotation from J. J. Stewart Perowne because I think it is a remarkable statement to be coming from a man who was liberal in his theology.

> The singer is in danger of his life; and timorous and faint-hearted counsellors would fain persuade him to seek safety in flight. But, full of unshaken faith in God, he rejects their counsel, believing that Jehovah, the righteous king, though He tries His servants, does not forsake them. Not the righteous, but the wicked have need to fear. The Psalm is so short and so general in its character, that it is not easy to say to what circumstances in David's life it should be referred. The choice seems, however, to lie between his persecution by Saul and the rebellion of his son Absalom. Delitzsch decides for the last, and thinks the counsel (v. 1), "flee to your mountain," comes from the mouth of friends who are anxious to persuade the king to betake himself, as he had before done when hunted by Saul, to "the rocks of the wild goats" (1 Sam. 24:2). It is in favor, to some extent, of this view that the expression in v. 3, "when the foundations are destroyed," points to a time when lawful authority was subverted. (*The Book of Psalms*, p. 166)

This is one time when I agree with a liberal. I think this psalm has reference to the time he fled from Absalom.

Here is another expression from the heart of this great king:

**In the LORD put I my trust: how say ye to my soul, Flee as
a bird to your mountain? [Ps. 11:1].**

This is the advice psychologists will give you today. They will tell you
that what you need to do is get away from your problems. Go off
somewhere—what you need is a rest. Flee from your present circumstances, as a bird to the mountain. My friend, getting away from it all
does not solve a thing. Years ago, in my southland, the lady of the
house was complaining to her wonderful housekeeper about wanting
to get away from it all. Her housekeeper said, "What are you trying to
get away from? This beautiful home? Your lovely children? Your wonderful husband? No matter where you go, you are going to have to lug
yourself along." You can never run away from yourself. How true that
is! People would tell David, "Flee as a bird to your mountain," but that
was not the way to solve his problems.

In our mechanical society and very monotonous culture it is very
tiring to sit in an automobile for seven hours on a freeway. Flying in an
airplane is a wonderful experience; but after you have been across the
country and around the world, flying gets monotonous. You are way
up in the air where there is not much to see or do. Actually, I think it is
a good thing for a person to get away from the busy life and the noise
of the city and the traffic to find a restful place to relax. But if you are
trying to run away from your *problems* or from some situation that you
ought to face, this is not good advice. You should not run away because of fear. Many who were counseling David to run away and to get
out of the country were afraid for his life, because Absalom, this son
of his, was trying to kill him.

**For, lo, the wicked bend their bow, they make ready
their arrow upon the string, that they may privily shoot
at the upright in heart [Ps. 11:2].**

Those who were following Absalom were willing to kill David if they
had the opportunity. There was great bitterness on both sides. When
Absalom came in battle against his father, David did not leave the

land. David retreated in order to reconnoiter and then came against his son with his army. David gave specific instructions to his three captains: "Remember my boy Absalom and don't harm him. I want him safe." Absalom made a big mistake in fighting his father and the veterans who were with him, because David was a seasoned warrior and knew all the tricks of the trade. He knew how to fight in the woods and the mountains. Absalom and his men were not as experienced, and they lost. Not only was there bitterness on Absalom's side, it was also on David's side—although not in David's heart—but Joab, one of David's captains, when he had the opportunity, put a dart through the boy and killed him. There was bitterness on both sides.

The death of his son broke David's heart. I don't think he ever recovered from that. When Absalom tried to take over, David fled from Jerusalem. Law and order had disappeared. No longer was there worship of the living and true God.

If the foundations be destroyed, what can the righteous do? [Ps. 11:3].

This is still a good question to ask. Today the authority of the Word of God is being challenged on every hand. As I write, we have the "new morality," which is sin that the Bible has condemned from the very beginning. The problem is, What can the righteous do? I will tell you what they can do. Listen to the psalmist:

The Lord is in his holy temple, the Lord's throne is in heaven: his eyes behold, his eyelids try, the children of men [Ps. 11:4].

God is watching us today. He is testing us. And the only place we can turn is to Him. When the foundations are taken out from under us, the righteous have God to cling to.

Abraham reached that place. When it says that Abraham believed God, it means that Abraham threw his arms around God and just held on. He believed God. And these are days when we can believe God and hold on to Him. It is time for many of us who cannot sing the Hallelujah Chorus to at least say it. How wonderful is our God!

The LORD trieth the righteous: but the wicked and him that loveth violence his soul hateth [Ps. 11:5].

"The LORD trieth the righteous" is better translated "the Lord *tests* the righteous." God knows who are His own, and He will test His children. He tests me and He may be testing you. And that doesn't mean He hates us. He is testing us for our good and His glory.

"But the wicked and him that loveth violence his soul hateth." If you think God is just lovey-dovey, you had better read this and some of the other psalms again. God hates the wicked who hold on to their wickedness. I don't think God loves the devil. I think God hates him, and He hates those who have no intention of turning to Him. Frankly, I do not like this distinction that I hear today that, "God loves the sinner, but He hates the sin." God has loved you so much that He gave His Son to die for you; but if you persist in your sin and continue in that sin, you are the enemy of God. And God is your enemy. God wants to save you, and He will save you if you turn to Him and forsake your iniquity. Until then, may I say, God is not a lovey-dovey, sentimental, old gentleman from Georgia.

Upon the wicked he shall rain snares, fire and brimstone, and an horrible tempest: this shall be the portion of their cup [Ps. 11:6].

The cup of iniquity is filling up in our day. And God is allowing it to fill up; He is doing nothing to hinder it. The wicked are prospering. He makes it rain on the unjust as well as the just. In fact, it looks to me like they are getting more rain than anybody else. This is *their* day.

For the righteous LORD loveth righteousness; his countenance doth behold the upright [Ps. 11:7].

The Lord *loves* righteousness. In time of trouble when the foundations are removed, we are to look from earth to heaven—the upright will behold His face. What a wonderful picture this is!

PSALM 12

THEME: *The godly in the midst of the godlessness of the Great Tribulation*

Prophetically, this psalm is like the preceding ones. It refers ultimately in its final fulfillment to the days of the Tribulation which will come upon Israel's godly remnant—also upon godly Gentiles—in that day.

In the opening verses we find a description of the apostasy in those days. You see, there is to be an apostasy in Israel as well as in the church.

Help, LORD; for the godly man ceaseth; for the faithful fail from among the children of men [Ps. 12:1].

It is easy to develop an Elijah complex today and say, "I am the only one left. I am the only one standing for God today." Many people develop that complex. It is not accurate, but it can happen when you see godlessness on every hand.

They speak vanity every one with his neighbour: with flattering lips and with a double heart do they speak [Ps. 12:2].

This is a day when Christians need to speak the truth. That is, we should not say one thing to a man's face and another thing when his back is turned. That is double-talk. It is being two-faced.

The LORD shall cut off all flattering lips, and the tongue that speaketh proud things:

Who have said, With our tongue will we prevail; our lips are our own: who is lord over us? [Ps. 12:3–4].

The psalmist goes after the proud in this psalm. They say, "We are going to say what we please." We are seeing that apostasy in the church is noted by pride like this. Jude predicted the coming apostasy, "These are murmurers, complainers, walking after their own lusts; and their mouth speaketh great swelling words, having men's persons in admiration because of advantage" (Jude 16). In other words, those in apostasy are a bunch of liars.

Now we see those who are God's people.

For the oppression of the poor, for the sighing of the needy, now will I arise, saith the LORD; I will set him in safety from him that puffeth at him [Ps. 12:5].

Or, better, the Lord says, "I will set him in safety at whom they puff." Today the enemy huffs and puffs like the wolf did in the story of the three little pigs. Two little pigs lost their homes because the big bad wolf blew them down. But the last little pig had a house that stood up under the huffing and puffing. The story of the three little pigs illustrates what David is saying here. God says, "I will set him in safety at whom they puff. I will hide him in the clefts of the rocks. I will put him in a place of safety."

The words of the LORD are pure words: as silver tried in a furnace of earth, purified seven times [Ps. 12:6].

Now the wicked boast and use flattery. You cannot believe what they say. But the words of the Lord are pure. That is one reason why we need to spend more time in the Word of God. It is the fortress into which God wants to put us.

Thou shalt keep them, O LORD, thou shalt preserve them from this generation for ever.

The wicked walk on every side, when the vilest men are exalted [Ps. 12:7–8].

We are living in a day like this, and it will be especially true during the time of the Great Tribulation. Listen to the prophet Isaiah when he says, "Hear the word of the LORD, ye that tremble at his word; Your brethren that hated you, that cast you out for my name's sake, said, Let the LORD be glorified [they said that in mockery]: but he shall appear to your joy, and they shall be ashamed" (Isa. 66:5). This is a wonderful picture given to us which describes the temple worship in Jerusalem at, I think, the end of the age. The Lord Jesus said in His day, when the enemy came to arrest Him, ". . . this is your hour, and the power of darkness" (Luke 22:53). We go through times when the enemy has the upper hand, but God won't let something happen to His own unless it will accomplish some worthwhile purpose in their hearts and lives.

PSALM 13

THEME: David's desperate plight

This is a rather doleful section of the Book of Psalms. As we have said, Psalm 9 through Psalm 15 deal with that time of trouble which is coming—the Great Tribulation—and ones who figure during this time: Antichrist, and the Jewish remnant which will be true to God. It will be a time of great testing.

David has written this psalm out of his own trying experience, but it has a contemporary interpretation. Also it has a prophetic or chronological interpretation, reaching down into the end times after the church is removed from the earth.

David is being pursued as he writes this psalm—probably by King Saul. He may have been hiding at this time in the cave of Adullam while the Philistines were teamed up to hunt him out. Day after day he found himself in a desperate situation. In weariness of body and soreness of mind and heart he cries out to God:

> **How long wilt thou forget me, O Lord? for ever? how long wilt thou hide thy face from me? [Ps. 13:1].**

David sounds extremely pessimistic here. He feels that God has forsaken him, that he is on his own. What you have here, as Delitzsch describes it, is a long, deep sigh. "It comes finally from a relieved breast, by an already much more gentle and half-calmed prayer."

> **How long shall I take counsel in my soul, having sorrow in my heart daily? how long shall mine enemy be exalted over me? [Ps. 13:2].**

David is asking, "How long will this continue?" At this time David is a very weary man. Then he turns in prayer to God. This is his resource and his recourse.

> **Consider and hear me, O LORD my God: lighten mine
> eyes, lest I sleep the sleep of death [Ps. 13:3].**

David was in grave danger when he wrote this. He was afraid to go to sleep for fear that his enemy would kill him. Yet, he needed rest badly. So he asked the Lord to protect and give him sleep.

> **Lest mine enemy say, I have prevailed against him; and
> those that trouble me rejoice when I am moved [Ps.
> 13:4].**

The enemy would rejoice if he could get to David. The rejoicing of the enemy would not only be against David but also against God, so he prays that the enemy will not get the upper hand. After having heaved this awful sigh of sorrow, he continues in prayer, and he finally settles back in wonderful faith and trust in God. This is a beautiful psalm.

> **But I have trusted in thy mercy; my heart shall rejoice in
> thy salvation [Ps. 13:5].**

David did not think he was smart enough to get out of his predicament on his own. He took precautions, of course, but he knew only God could deliver him. God was his salvation.

> **I will sing unto the LORD, because he hath dealt bounti-
> fully with me [Ps. 13:6].**

My friend, wherever you are and whoever you are and however you are, you can still sing praises to God. As I write this, it is easy for me to praise Him. I just got a good report from my doctor about my physical condition. The Lord has been good to me and it is easy to praise Him, but I think of a man in Southern California who for years ignored God. Then he was stricken with cancer. He is flat on his back, but he has turned to the Lord through our radio program. Although he is in bad condition, a friend of mine who visited him told me, "It will rejoice your heart and humble you to visit this man and to see that in the midst of trouble he talks about how good God has been to him, how God has saved him, and how wonderful He is." When you can praise God in a spot like that, you have arrived. He may be farther along than I am.

And so in this psalm we have seen the desperate plight of David which mirrors the plight of God's people in the Great Tribulation.

PSALM 14

THEME: Depravity of man in the last days—atheistic, filthy, rebellious

This psalm is linked to the other psalms, especially Psalm 12. In that psalm you will recall that we saw the corruption of the last days. The godly man had ceased, it seemed; and the godless were in control. Corruption, wickedness, and lawlessness abounded. You may think it is a picture of this day, but if I may use the common colloquialism of the street, "You ain't seen nothin' yet." Wait until the Great Tribulation comes. By the way, I hope you don't see it, because God's own—those who are in the body of believers—are not going through the Great Tribulation. He has already said that He would keep them from "the hour of temptation, which shall come upon all the world, to try them that dwell upon the earth" (Rev. 3:10). The church, by which I mean the true believers, will leave before that time. This psalm certainly sets before us the corruption and wickedness of the last days, the end of the age.

Notice the marvelous arrangement of this psalm made by Bishop Horne. He divides this psalm into three parts: the corruption of the world, the enmity against the people of God, and the longing and prayer for salvation. This is the picture of Psalm 14. It is brief but very important.

THE CORRUPTION OF THE WORLD

The fool hath said in his heart, There is no God. They are corrupt, they have done abominable works, there is none that doeth good [Ps. 14:1].

The Hebrew word for "fool" in this verse is *nabal*. This may ring a bell in your thinking, because there was a man by the name of Nabal who was married to a lovely woman by the name of Abigail. His story is told in 1 Samuel 25. His name certainly characterized him accurately. He acted a fool. The word *nabal* may be translated "simple, silly, simpleton, fool, or madman."

I have a very intelligent friend who has been very successful in dealing with atheists. He was in a group of men one day when an atheist said, "I don't believe there is a God. Man doesn't have a soul, and when he dies, he dies like a dog." This man went on raving like a madman. My friend waited until the group began to break up and then approached this man. He said, "I understand you said that you are an atheist." Upon hearing these words the man launched into another tirade about his belief that there is no God. My friend said, "I would like to ask you a question. The Bible says, 'The fool hath said in his heart, There is no God.' The word *fool* means insane or mad. Either you were not sincere when you talked about God as you did and you were just talking for the benefit of the crowd, or you are a fool and a madman. I would like to know which one it is." The man turned and walked away. Knowing what we do about the universe today, only a madman would say that there is no God. Man has found that the universe works more accurately than any clock or watch he has been able to make. And there is no watch running around that "just happened"—some watchmaker made it. The universe that is timed more accurately than a watch tells us that there is a universe-maker. The *fool* has said in his heart that there is no God, and now the fool begins to appear on the scene. We have already had a glimpse of him in Psalm 10:4, where we read, "God is not in all his thoughts." A better translation of this is, "All of his thoughts are, 'There is no God!'" He exhibits the very depth of human depravity.

There are many people with Ph.D.s teaching in our universities today. Many of them are atheists. I want to say this carefully—the lowest that a man can sink in human depravity is to be an atheist. That is what the Word of God says. If you do not believe there is a God, you are a madman; you are crazy. You do not have any real sense. Having a high I.Q. is not enough. I used to teach with a man who had a Ph.D., and he didn't have sense enough to get out of the rain. I played golf with him one day when it began to rain. He looked at me and asked, "What shall we do?" He was really asking for information. What would any sensible person do when it starts pouring down rain? I said to him, "I think we had better get in out of the rain!" Even I knew that, but he didn't seem to know. So, you see, a scholastic degree doesn't prove a man's intelligence! "They are corrupt, they have done abominable works, there is none that doeth good." I believe you will find that most atheists are also great sinners. Gross immorality is generally one of their characteristics. A man who mixes with the college set told me, "It is amazing the number of Ph.D.s who claim to be atheists and who are living in gross immorality. And some of them actually live in filth—and I mean material, physical filth."

> **The LORD looked down from heaven upon the children of men, to see if there were any that did understand, and seek God [Ps. 14:2].**

And what did He find?

> **They are all gone aside, they are all together become filthy: there is none that doeth good, no, not one [Ps. 14:3].**

Paul quotes this verse in Romans 3:12, "They are all gone out of the way, they are together become unprofitable; there is none that doeth good, no, not one." Paul is not only speaking about atheists; he is speaking about everyone. This is a picture of you and me, friend. I am not an atheist, and I don't imagine you are, but we are sinners. We do not do good. The condition of man is corrupt, and the first three verses tell us the depths to which man can go.

ENMITY AGAINST THE PEOPLE OF GOD

They are not only against God, but they are against the people of God.

Have all the workers of iniquity no knowledge? who eat
up my people as they eat bread, and call not upon the
LORD.

There were they in great fear: for God is in the generation of the righteous.

Ye have shamed the counsel of the poor, because the
LORD is his refuge [Ps. 14:4–6].

There is a lot of pretense upon the part of rich politicians today. A
college professor, who is a friend of mine and who is liberal in his
theology and in his politics, calls these politicians "limousine liberals." He said, "They don't know anything about what the *poor* man
goes through, and yet they pretend to be liberal." They are like the rich
man who always lets some crumbs fall off his table for the poor man to
keep him satisfied (see Luke 16:20–21). I find no rich man today
giving up his riches to help the poor. What little you and I accumu-
late he will tax to death; yet he somehow escapes taxation himself.
God certainly knows human nature, does He not? This is a picture of
them.

THE LONGING AND PRAYER FOR SALVATION

Now here is a note of triumph.

Oh that the salvation of Israel were come out of Zion!
when the LORD bringeth back the captivity of his people,
Jacob shall rejoice, and Israel shall be glad [Ps. 14:7].

This verse looks forward in anticipation to that glorious day when out
of Zion will come salvation for Israel. In that day Jacob shall rejoice
and Israel shall be glad. You cannot misunderstand this verse. Anyone who says that God does not have a future purpose for Israel is
admitting that he doesn't know very much about the Psalms. He may

try to avoid what is so clearly stated in other passages of the Word, but how can he deny that the heart cry and the joy of the psalmist is in the future when God establishes a kingdom on earth with Israel at the center?

PSALM 15

THEME: *Description of those who will be in the presence of God*

This is another brief psalm which will conclude the section which began with Psalm 9. If you review these psalms you will see a definite development. Psalms 9 and 10 picture Satan's man, who is characterized by pride, boasting, and self-sufficiency. Psalm 11 deals with the testing of the righteous. In Psalm 12 we see the godly in the midst of godlessness and the ultimate godlessness of the Great Tribulation. Psalm 13 mirrors the plight of God's people in the Great Tribulation. Psalm 14 shows us the depravity of man in the last days, with his atheistic attitude and his filthy and rebellious ways. Now Psalm 15 tells us about those who shall enter the kingdom. It describes those who are going to be in the presence of Jehovah.

LORD, who shall abide in thy tabernacle? who shall dwell in thy holy hill? [Ps. 15:1].

There is only one holy hill; the Bible calls it Zion, which is in the land of Israel. He is talking about those who will enter the millennial kingdom, the kingdom Christ will establish on earth with Israel as the center.

He that walketh uprightly, and worketh righteousness, and speaketh the truth in his heart.

He that backbiteth not with his tongue, nor doeth evil to his neighbour, nor taketh up a reproach against his neighbour.

In whose eyes a vile person is contemned; but he honoureth them that fear the LORD. He that sweareth to his own hurt, and changeth not [Ps. 15:2-4].

"In whose eyes a vile person is contemned"—that is, despised. In our contemporary culture the opposite is often true; the vile person is honored, and the godly man is despised.

"He that sweareth to his own hurt, and changeth not" means that he will go on record for the truth and will not change his story to protect himself.

> **He that putteth not out his money to usury, nor taketh reward against the innocent. He that doeth these things shall never be moved [Ps. 15:5].**

In this psalm David is saying exactly what James said: "Yea, a man may say, Thou hast faith, and I have works: shew me thy faith without thy works, and I will shew thee my faith by my works" (James 2:18). I like the way John Calvin put it: "Faith alone saves, but faith that saves is not alone." Who is going to stand before God? Those who have had a faith in God that has produced a life of righteousness. At the time I write this, there is a great deal of talk about the soon coming of Christ, and yet I don't see much change in the lives of folk who say they are expecting Him. My friend, if you really believe Jesus is coming soon—or even if you believe you will someday stand before Him to give an account, you will make sure that you live your life in such a way that it will count for God. This is the real test that will prove whether or not you love Him and look for Jesus' return.

This is a tremendous psalm!

PSALM 16

THEME: *The resurrection of the Messiah*

Psalms 16 through 24 form another segment that belongs together. In our songbooks today songs of like themes are grouped together—songs of praise, songs of repentance, etc., are in certain sections of our books. Well, this is how the Psalms are arranged in this songbook. The theme of these nine psalms is the prophecy of Christ blended with the prophecy of the faithful remnant.

Psalm 16 gives us the song of resurrection. This is the third messianic psalm. It touches on the life of Christ (v. 8), the death of Christ (v. 9), the resurrection of Christ (v. 10), and the ascension of Christ (v. 11). The resurrection of Christ is quoted from this psalm in the New Testament in three different places.

This psalm is called a "Michtam of David." The word *Michtam* is of uncertain origin. Martin Luther translated it as "a golden jewel," which I think is close to the actual meaning. Psalms 56 through 60 are also called Michtam psalms.

The messianic meaning of this psalm is fully established by the testimony of the Holy Spirit in the New Testament, as we shall see.

Let us call this psalm the *Golden Jewel of David* because he is looking forward to the One coming in his line, the One of whom he could say, "This is all my salvation."

> **Preserve me, O God: for in thee do I put my trust [Ps. 16:1].**

This reveals the wonderful voice of the Lord Jesus Christ when He said He had come to do the Father's will and had committed Himself completely to the Father (John 5:30). Christ purposely took a place of subjection on earth when He took upon Himself our humanity. Little man—and all of us are pretty little—becomes proud and tries to lift himself up. We have men in high positions today—politicians, statesmen, men of science, educators, and ministers, who almost take the place of God. But actually we are pretty small potatoes here on this earth. We don't amount to much. We were created lower than the angels (Heb. 2:6–7). I *have* to take that position, but Christ did not have to take it. He *willingly* became man. I am glad that I am a man, but I also need to recognize what man really is. I rejoice in what God is going to do for me, and with me, and to all those who believe in Him.

The psalmist says, "Preserve me, O God: for in thee do I put my trust." What a picture of the Lord Jesus Christ! It was a picture of David, and I trust it is also a picture of you and me.

O my soul, thou hast said unto the Lord, Thou art my Lord: my goodness extendeth not to thee [Ps. 16:2].

Have you ever ridden along in your car, walked in the mountains or by the seashore, looked up and said, "You are my Creator, my Redeemer, and my Lord"? Have you ever told Him that? I have a little grandson, and you cannot imagine what it means to an old man to have his grandson crawl up in his lap, put his little arms around him, and say, "You are my grandpa." It is quite wonderful. And we have a heavenly Father who made us in His image, and I am of the opinion He likes us to come to Him and tell Him, "You are my Lord." Have you told Him that lately? Don't be like the proud people spoken of in Matthew 7:22–23: "Many will say to me in that day, Lord, Lord, have we not prophesied in thy name? and in thy name have cast out devils? and in thy name done many wonderful works? And then will I profess unto them, I never knew you: depart from me, ye that work iniquity." These people called Him "Lord" and did not even know Him. When I call Him "Lord," I want to *mean* it.

But to the saints that are in the earth, and to the excellent, in whom is all my delight [Ps. 16:3].

You see, He is the Lord to His saints on the earth—this privilege does not extend to everybody, as the next verse indicates.

Their sorrows shall be multiplied that hasten after another god: their drink offerings of blood will I not offer, nor take up their names into my lips [Ps. 16:4].

"Their sorrows shall be multiplied that hasten after another . . ." (you will notice that "god" is in italics in most Bibles because the word was supplied by the translators). It means that they "hasten after another" whom they think is God.

What a picture this is. The pagan had what he called his gods; in David's day they were Dagon and Baal. I am amused at folk who say they have no creed. A man said to me, "I don't believe in having a creed." I replied, "Yes, you do. Your creed is that you don't believe in having any creed." You cannot help but have a creed.

There used to be a church in downtown Los Angeles that had one whole side exposed to the street. On it there was a sign which said, "No creed, but Christ." Well, that was their creed and a good one, although it was oversimplification, and they weren't quite telling the truth to make a statement like that.

The Lord is the portion of mine inheritance and of my cup: thou maintainest my lot.

The lines are fallen unto me in pleasant places; yea, I have a goodly heritage [Ps. 16:5-6].

How wonderful—"the Lord is the portion of mine inheritance." The Lord came to earth and took His place, walking in a world of sin and sorrow. He was a perfect stranger down here. He rejoiced in Jehovah. There was peace and joy in His life.

He said, "My portion and my cup." What is the difference between a "portion" and a "cup"? My portion is what belongs to me—whether or not I enjoy it—it's mine. My cup is what I actually appropriate and make my own. For example, what is put on my grandson's plate at the dinner table is his portion. But frankly, he scatters it around and does not eat all of it; he only appropriates so much. He has a "portion" given to him, but his "cup" is what he actually consumes.

Many people in the world who have been blessed by God with all spiritual blessings do not enjoy them. Their cups do not run over. They don't have much in their cups. God wants us to *enjoy* life. Jesus said, ". . . I am come that they might have life, and that they might have it more abundantly" (John 10:10). He also said, "These things have I spoken unto you, that my joy might remain in you, and that your *joy* might be *full*" (John 15:11). Some of us have a little fun sometimes but not all the time. We need to be full of life and joy all of the time.

> **I will bless the LORD, who hath given me counsel: my reins also instruct me in the night seasons [Ps. 16:7].**

What do you think about at night when you cannot sleep? The psalmist thought about the Lord.

Now we come to the verses that are quoted in the New Testament.

> **I have set the LORD always before me: because he is at my right hand, I shall not be moved.**

> **Therefore my heart is glad, and my glory rejoiceth: my flesh also shall rest in hope.**

> **For thou wilt not leave my soul in hell: neither wilt thou suffer thine Holy One to see corruption [Ps. 16:8–10].**

This is the psalm of the resurrection of Jesus Christ. This was the heart of Peter's message on the day of Pentecost. "For David speaketh concerning him, I foresaw the Lord always before my face, for he is on my right hand, that I should not be moved: Therefore did my heart rejoice, and my tongue was glad; moreover also my flesh shall rest in hope: Because thou wilt not leave my soul in hell [*sheol* was the Hebrew word, meaning "the unseen world"], neither wilt thou suffer thine Holy One to see corruption. Thou hast made known to me the ways of life; thou shalt make me full of joy with thy countenance. Men and brethren, let me freely speak unto you of the patriarch David, that he is both dead and buried, and his sepulchre is with us unto this day [from where Peter was preaching in the temple area, they could see the tomb of David, and Peter undoubtedly pointed to it]. Therefore being a prophet, and knowing that God had sworn with an oath to him, that of the fruit of his loins, according to the flesh, he would raise up Christ to sit on his throne; He seeing this before spake of the resurrection of Christ, that his soul was not left in hell, neither his flesh did see corruption" (Acts 2:25-31). Peter said clearly that Psalm 16:8-10 spoke of the resurrection of Christ. There are several liberal expositors—Perowne is one of them—who say that Psalm 16 has no reference to the resurrection of Christ. When a liberal makes that statement, I have to consider what Simon Peter said. When Peter preached on the day of Pentecost, several thousand people turned to Christ and were saved, which brought about a revolution in the Roman Empire. With this in mind I feel like saying to the liberals, "How many are coming to the Lord through your ministry?" That is the real test. Simon Peter said that Psalm 16 refers to the resurrection of Jesus Christ, and I am taking his word for it.

Peter also said more on the day of Pentecost: "This Jesus hath God raised up, whereof we all are witnesses. Therefore being by the right hand of God exalted, and having received of the Father the promise of the Holy Ghost, he hath shed forth this, which ye now see and hear. For David is not ascended into the heavens: but he saith himself, The LORD said unto my Lord, Sit thou on my right hand, Until I make thy foes thy footstool. Therefore let all the house of Israel know assuredly, that God hath made that same Jesus, whom ye have crucified, both Lord and Christ" (Acts 2:32-36). Obviously Psalm 16 refers to the resurrection of the Lord Jesus Christ.

Paul also quoted from this psalm. In Acts 13:35-37 he says, "Wherefore he saith also in another psalm, Thou shalt not suffer thine Holy One to see corruption. For David, after he had served his own generation by the will of God, fell on sleep, and was laid unto his fathers, and saw corruption: But he, whom God raised again, saw no corruption." You see, Paul also said it was the psalm of Jesus' resurrection.

What we have in this psalm is quite remarkable. In verse 8 we have the life of Christ. "I have set the LORD always before me: because he is at my right hand, I shall not be moved." That, my friend, was the pathway He followed down here, and it is the pathway I want to follow.

Then in verse 9 we have the death of Christ: "Therefore my heart is glad, and my glory rejoiceth: my flesh also shall rest in hope." He died there upon the cross, knowing that God would raise Him from the dead.

Then we have the resurrection of Christ in verse 10: "For thou wilt not leave my soul in hell [that is, the grave]; neither wilt thou suffer thine Holy One to see corruption."

Then we have the ascension of Christ in verse 11:

Thou wilt shew me the path of life: in thy presence is fulness of joy; at thy right hand there are pleasures for evermore [Ps. 16:11].

As you can see, this is a wonderful resurrection psalm, and it is so used in the New Testament. The resurrection of Christ is definitely prophesied in this great messianic psalm.

PSALM 17

THEME: A prayer of David when in great danger

Psalm 17 is entitled, "A Prayer of David." The question is, When was it written? It seems to be a prayer that came out of his wilderness experience. It probably concerns the time when Saul and his men were almost upon him and came close to taking him. This psalm reveals David's trust in God, but in the final analysis it speaks primarily of the Lord Jesus Christ. This psalm can also be a prayer for us today when we find ourselves in similar situations of trial, anxiety, or danger. As we study this psalm, keep in mind that we are in a new series that speaks of Christ in prophecy. After all, this is a HIM book; it is all about Him.

> **Hear the right, O Lord, attend unto my cry, give ear unto my prayer, that goeth not out of feigned lips [Ps. 17:1].**

This is a prayer of David—probably when he is being pursued by Saul—and his life is in danger. This prayer comes from his heart, and he says what he is really thinking. There will be no "put-on" in it; he is not going to speak with "feigned lips." In other words, there will be no insincerity in what he is saying.

> **Let my sentence come forth from thy presence; let thine eyes behold the things that are equal [Ps. 17:2].**

He is willing for the Lord to balance things off. "Let thine eyes behold the things that are equal." I don't know about you, but I am not asking for justice from God; I am asking for mercy. What most of us need from Him is mercy.

> **Thou hast proved mine heart; thou hast visited me in the night; thou hast tried me, and shalt find nothing; I**

am purposed that my mouth shall not transgress [Ps.
17:3].

It is interesting to note that when God tested David, He *did* find something and, when He tested me, He also found something. I have a
notion that when He tested you, He found something also. These
words must first of all be applied to Christ.

When the psalmist speaks in verse 1 of the prayer that did not go
out of "feigned lips," it is a perfect picture of our perfect Lord. Peter
says of the Lord, "Who did no sin, neither was guile found in his
mouth" (1 Pet. 2:22). Peter goes on to say about Him, "Who, when he
was reviled, reviled not again; when he suffered, he threatened not;
but committed himself to him that judgeth righteously" (1 Pet. 2:23).

**Concerning the works of men, by the word of thy lips I
have kept me from the paths of the destroyer [Ps. 17:4].**

The "destroyer" is none other than Satan. Because of his presence in
the world, every child of God should be alert. David was in enemy
territory, and he was aware of that when he was hiding from Saul. And
we are in enemy territory—the earth is Satan's bailiwick. To the
church in Pergamos the Lord said, "I know thy works, and where thou
dwellest, even where Satan's seat [Satan's throne] is . . ." (Rev. 2:13). I
don't know where you live today, but some of us think that Satan's
throne is very close to Los Angeles.

Our Lord didn't fall into Satan's trap as we often do.

**Hold up my goings in thy paths, that my footsteps slip
not.**

**I have called upon thee, for thou wilt hear me, O God:
incline thine ear unto me, and hear my speech [Ps.
17:5–6].**

Delitzsch translates verse 6 like this: "As such an one I call upon thee,
and thou hearest me." David knew he was heard. The Lord Jesus

Christ identified Himself with His own. When He prayed, God heard Him. We can be sure, my friend, that He hears and answers our prayers when we are in trouble.

> **Shew thy marvellous loving-kindness, O thou that savest by thy right hand them which put their trust in thee from those that rise up against them.**
>
> **Keep me as the apple of the eye, hide me under the shadow of thy wings [Ps. 17:7–8].**

Years before God had used a similar expression when He said to Israel, "Ye have seen what I did unto the Egyptians, and how I bare you on eagles' wings, and brought you unto myself" (Exod. 19:4). This is a picture of where we are placed—in the shadow of His wings. Years later the Lord Jesus said of Jerusalem: "O Jerusalem, Jerusalem, thou that killest the prophets, and stonest them which are sent unto thee, how often would I have gathered thy children together, even as a hen gathereth her chickens under her wings, and ye would not!" (Matt. 23:37). Notice it is "under her wings"—this is also the picture David is giving us.

> **From the wicked that oppress me, from my deadly enemies, who compass me about.**
>
> **They are enclosed in their own fat: with their mouth they speak proudly.**
>
> **They have now compassed us in our steps: they have set their eyes bowing down to the earth;**
>
> **Like as a lion that is greedy of his prey, and as it were a young lion lurking in secret places [Ps. 17:9–12].**

David is crying out to God. He knew that God had heard his prayer.

> **Arise, O Lord, disappoint him, cast him down: deliver my soul from the wicked, which is thy sword:**

From men which are thy hand, O LORD, from men of the
world, which have their portion in this life, and whose
belly thou fillest with thy hid treasure: they are full of
children, and leave the rest of their substance to their
babes.

As for me, I will behold thy face in righteousness: I shall
be satisfied, when I awake, with thy likeness [Ps.
17:13–15].

Here is David, hiding in a cave, and he calls out to God to deliver him.
David knows that God is going to deliver him and that one day he will
be in His presence. At the moment, however, the enemy seems to be so
strong and powerful.

You and I as God's children look out on a world that is against us.
We are like the little boy playing in a vacant lot who saw a big old
weed growing there and decided to pull it out of the ground. As he
was pulling, a man happened by, stopped, and watched him. The little fellow would pull on one side and grunt, then get on the other side
and pull. Finally, with one great supreme effort the little fellow
pulled, the roots of the weed gave way, and he fell back with a bump.
For a few moments he sat there shocked. The man who had been
watching him said, "Son, that was a mighty big pull." The boy replied, "It sure was 'cause the whole world was pulling against me."
My friend, that is the position of the child of God today, but we have a
resource and a recourse by coming to our Heavenly Father. This is
what our Lord did when He was on earth, and so did David when he
was in real danger.

What a psalm to help those who are in trouble today—especially
when we find we have enemies who are against us. Most of us who
stand for God have enemies—we have enemies just like a dog has
fleas! They seem to be a part of the Christian's life.

PSALM 18

THEME: David's praise when God delivered him from the hand of Saul

This is another wonderful psalm written by David. Many of the liberal expositors have found nothing in this psalm but David's experience, and they have said some wonderful things about it. I would like to quote from Perowne as an example:

> In this magnificent hymn the royal poet sketches in a few grand outlines the tale of his life—the record of his marvelous deliverances and of the victories which Jehovah had given him—the record, too, of his own heart, the truth of his affection towards God, and the integrity of purpose by which it had ever been influenced. Throughout that singularly chequered life, hunted as he had been by Saul before he came to the throne, and harassed perpetually after he became king by rivals, who disputed his authority, and endeavored to steal away the hearts of his people—compelled to flee for his life before his own son, and engaged afterward in long and fierce wars with foreign nations—one thing had never forsaken him, the love and the presence of Jehovah. By His help he had subdued every enemy, and now, in his old age, looking backward with devout thankfulness on the past, he sings this great song of praise to the God of his life (*The Book of Psalms*, p. 192).

Everything this expositor has said is true; he has given the local, contemporary interpretation of this psalm. This psalm is a duplication of 2 Samuel 22; and, when we studied that book, I touched upon it lightly but will deal with the contents a little more closely here.

There is a deeper meaning to this psalm than the expositor gave us. Some of the utterances that are called poetic figures are more than figures of speech. These utterances speak of the Son of God, the Anointed One of God, Christ our Savior in His sufferings. Someone has labeled this psalm "All the way from the jaws of death to Jehovah's throne."

We are living today in a world where a lot is said about love, and many think the subject of love is foreign to the Old Testament. Notice how this psalm opens:

I will love thee, O Lord, my strength [Ps. 18:1].

When was the last time you told the Lord you loved Him? To tell Him you love Him is one of the most wonderful things you can do. Praise toward God begins because He loves us and has provided a salvation for us. He preserves us and by His providence watches over us.

Notice that the Lord is called "my strength."

The Lord is my rock, and my fortress, and my deliverer; my God, my strength, in whom I will trust; my buckler, and the horn of my salvation, and my high tower [Ps. 18:2].

He calls the Lord his strength, his rock, his fortress, and his deliverer—in all of this He is his Savior, you see. Then he says again that He is his strength, He is his shield, his horn, and his high tower. He is my shield—He protects me. He is my horn, my power. By laying hold of the horns of the altar a person would be safe from his attackers. That is how we need to hold on to our God today. The Lord, our Savior, is our horn. He is our high tower. A high tower is also a good place for protection and a good place to get a vision and a perspective of life. Many of us need to go to the high tower. This verse contains excellent names for our God.

The word that interests me a great deal is the personal pronoun *my*. David says, "The Lord is *my* rock, and *my* fortress, and *my* deliverer." It is one thing to talk about the attributes of God and say He is omnipotent, but the important thing is to say He is *my* strength. It is one thing to say He is a shepherd. David could have said, "The Lord is *a* shepherd," and He is, but it is altogether different to say, "He is *my* shepherd."

I think I can illustrate what I am talking about. One day I went out to the airport to pick up my wife and grandson. She brought him back on a plane so that he would not have to travel from the East coast in a car. There were lots of little boys and girls at the airport. They were all precious children, and as I looked at them I smiled. Then all of a sudden here comes one that is different. Do you know what makes him different? He is *my* grandson. There were lots of grandparents there, and, oh, how sentimental we grandparents can become! Their grandchildren were just as special to them as mine was to me—all because of the little possessive pronoun *my*.

Can you say, "The Lord is *my* shepherd; He is *my* high tower; He is *my* horn; He is *my* shield; He is *my* strength; He is *my* deliverer; He is *my* rock; He is *my* fortress"?

I will call upon the LORD, who is worthy to be praised: so shall I be saved from mine enemies [Ps. 18:3].

Worship comes from the old Anglo-Saxon word *worth*. Worship is that which is extended to the one who is worthy. David sang, "I will call upon the LORD"—why? Because He "is worthy to be praised."

The sorrows of death compassed me, and the floods of ungodly men made me afraid [Ps. 18:4].

Once again the psalm reaches out and touches the Lord Jesus Christ. Bishop Horne saw something else in this psalm. Let me quote from him:

Let us suppose King Messiah, like His progenitor of old, is seated upon the throne. From thence let us imagine Him taking a retrospective view of the sufferings He had undergone, the battles He had fought and the victories He had gained. With this before our minds, we shall be able in some measure, to conceive the force of the words "With all the yearnings of affection I will love Thee, O Jehovah, My strength, through My union with whom I have finished My work, and am now exalted to praise Thee in those who are redeemed." Whenever we sing this Psalm, let us think we are singing it in conjunction with our Saviour, risen from the dead; a consideration, which surely will incite us to do it with becoming gratitude and devotion. (Quoted in A. C. Gaebelein, *The Book of Psalms*, p. 82)

What a picture! Friend, this happens to be a psalm we can join Him in singing.

Listen to him now, as he recounts his experiences—and I think this presents the life of David in a limited way, but more especially the life of the Lord Jesus who said, "The sorrows of death compassed me, the floods of ungodly men made me afraid."

> **The sorrows of hell [*Sheol*, the grave] compassed me about: the snares of death prevented [were round about] me.**
>
> **In my distress I called upon the LORD, and cried unto my God: he heard my voice out of his temple, and my cry came before him, even into his ears [Ps. 18:5–6].**

Notice again "my God." And what happened? God responded. And what happened when the Lord Jesus was brought back from the grave? The next few verses tell us. (In the following section the first person possessive pronoun changes to the third person, and it refers to the Lord.)

> **Then the earth shook and trembled; the foundations also of the hills moved and were shaken, because he was wroth [Ps. 18:7].**

He was angry with sinful men for what they had done to His Son. The Gospels tell us that when the stone was rolled away from the sepulchre there was an earthquake. What else took place in the heavens which corresponds to the following verses we do not know.

There went up a smoke out of his nostrils, and fire out of his mouth devoured: coals were kindled by it.

He bowed the heavens also, and came down: and darkness was under his feet.

And he rode upon a cherub, and did fly: yea, he did fly upon the wings of the wind.

He made darkness his secret place: his pavilion round about him were dark waters and thick clouds of the skies [Ps. 18:8–11].

There was darkness on the day that the Lord Jesus Christ was crucified. Who did all of this?

The LORD also thundered in the heavens, and the Highest gave his voice; hail stones and coals of fire [Ps. 18:13].

This psalm began using the pronoun *my*. Then it changed at verse 7 and talked about what God has done. Now in this next verse it is "He and me." That may be bad grammar, but that is the way it is here—He and me!

He sent from above, he took me, he drew me out of many waters.

He delivered me from my strong enemy, and from them which hated me: for they were too strong for me [Ps. 18:16–17].

"He delivered *me* from my strong enemy." Oh, how you and I need a personal, vital relationship with God! Let's come to grips with Him. He has delivered us from the enemy. Do you need help today? Do you need a partner today? I want to recommend One to you. He will never desert you. He will never leave you alone. He will never forsake you. He says, ". . . lo, I am with you alway, even unto the end of the world"

(Matt. 28:20). That is the reason that I depend on Him more than I depend on anyone. That is also the reason you should depend on Him instead of depending on any human being. Psalm 118:8 says, "It is better to trust in the Lord than to put confidence in man."

> **He delivereth me from mine enemies: yea, thou liftest me up above those that rise up against me: thou hast delivered me from the violent man [Ps. 18:48].**

"The violent man" I think is Satan.

> **Therefore will I give thanks unto thee, O Lord, among the heathen, and sing praises unto thy name.**
>
> **Great deliverance giveth he to his king; and sheweth mercy to his anointed, to David, and to his seed for evermore [Ps. 18:49–50].**

God extends His mercy to us today. This marvelous psalm closes on a note of praise to God. Oh, that there might be praise in your mouth and mine, in your life and mine, in your heart and mine, toward our God! Praise to God. "O give thanks unto the Lord, for he is good: for his mercy endureth for ever. Let the redeemed of the Lord say so" (Ps. 107:1–2). If the redeemed do not say the Lord is good, nobody else in the world will. The redeemed ought to say so. We need some "say-so" Christians.

PSALM 19

THEME: The revelation of God in His creation, in His commandments, and in Christ

This can be called a great psalm of creation. It has been divided by many scholars into two parts: creation and the revelation of Jehovah in the Law, that is, in His Word. I have attempted to divide the psalm into three parts: creation of the cosmos, the commandments, and Christ—I feel that He has a special place here in the subject of redemption, salvation, and the grace of God. We will find God revealed in His creation, in His commandments, and in His grace in Christ. This is all that God saw fit to give to man, and I do not think He has exhausted all the things He could tell us about Himself.

This is another psalm of David, and it is so called in the inspired text. Also there is a division right in the text: the first part (vv. 1–6) uses *El* for the name of God, meaning the "Mighty One." He is the Mighty One in creation—"In the beginning *Elohim* [*Elohim* is the plural of *El*] created the heavens and the earth" (see Gen. 1:1). *Elohim* is His name as the Creator. The second division begins at verse 7, "The law of the LORD is perfect"—and His name is Jehovah. It is so used seven times in this section, and the last time two other names are added, *Jehovah, Tzuri, Goeli,* meaning "Jehovah, my Rock, my Redeemer." Common sense scholarship does not try to explain the difference in names by contending that it was written by two different authors. If the same common sense had been used in the study of the Pentateuch, some scholars would not have come up with the "Jehovist and Elohist" writers of the Pentateuch theory. The same writer wrote it, using the two names for God. The Psalms flood light on many sections of the Bible. I trust they bless your heart and life.

GOD IN CREATION

This is a morning psalm. It speaks of creation in the first six verses. Psalm 8 was a creation psalm, and in it we saw the moon and the

stars. It was a night psalm. Psalm 19 is called a day psalm because it is
the sun that is brought before us.

> **The heavens declare the glory of God; and the firma-
> ment sheweth his handiwork.**
>
> **Day unto day uttereth speech, and night unto night
> sheweth knowledge.**
>
> **There is no speech nor language, where their voice is
> not heard.**
>
> **Their line is gone out through all the earth, and their
> words to the end of the world. In them hath he set a tab-
> ernacle for the sun.**
>
> **Which is as a bridegroom coming out of his chamber,
> and rejoiceth as a strong man to run a race.**
>
> **His going forth is from the end of the heaven, and his
> circuit unto the ends of it: and there is nothing hid from
> the heat thereof [Ps. 19:1–6].**

Now I want to share with you the translation made by Dr. Arno C.
Gaebelein, who was one of my teachers, and in whom I have great
confidence. He was well acquainted with the great Hebrew and Ger-
man scholars who made a thorough study of the Book of Psalms: "The
heavens declare the glory of God and the expanse maketh known the
work of His hands. Day unto day poureth forth speech, and night unto
night showeth knowledge—there is no speech and there are no words,
Yet their voice is heard. Their line is gone out through all the earth,
and to the end of the earth their words; in them hath He set a tent for
the sun. And he is as a bridegroom coming out of his chamber, He
rejoiceth as a strong man to run the course. His going forth is from the
end of the heavens, and his circuit unto the ends of them, and there is
nothing hid from the heat thereof" (*The Book of Psalms*, p. 89).

This is a marvelous psalm. "The heavens declare the glory of
God." Paul says it this way in Romans 1:20, "For the invisible things

of him from the creation of the world are clearly seen, being understood by the things that are made, even his eternal power and Godhead; so that they are without excuse." The heavens tell out the wisdom of God, they tell out the power of God, and they tell out, I think, something of the plan and purpose of God. From the beginning creation has been the primitive witness of God to man, His creature.

In all the creeds of the church, including the Apostles' Creed, creation is ascribed exclusively to God the Father. But when you come to the New Testament, where there is an amplification even of the act of creation, you find that it is not exactly accurate to say that God the Father is the Maker of heaven and earth. The Trinity was involved in the creation of the earth. In fact, the word *Elohim* is a plural word in the Hebrew, and it speaks of the Trinity. The New Testament tells us that the Lord Jesus was the agent of creation, and the Holy Spirit came in and refurbished and revamped it: ". . . the Spirit of God moved upon the face of the waters" (Gen. 1:2). The apostle John tells of another beginning: "In the beginning was the Word, and the Word was with God, and the Word was God. . . . All things were made by him; and without him was not any thing made that was made" (John 1:1–3). This is the Lord Jesus Christ. Colossians 1:16, speaking about the Lord Jesus, says, "For by him were all things created, that are in heaven, and that are in earth, visible and invisible, whether they be thrones, or dominions, or principalities, or powers: all things were created by him, and for him." The Lord Jesus was the agent in creation. The first chapter of Ephesians tells us that all the members of the Trinity were involved in our redemption: God the Father planned it, the Son paid for it, and the Holy Spirit protects it. This applies to God's creation as well: God the Father planned this universe; the Son carried out the plan, and He is the One who redeemed it; and the Holy Spirit today is moving and brooding over this creation.

It is interesting to note that the sun is prominent and likened to a bridegroom coming out of his chamber. When I was in Jerusalem, every morning I could see the sun come up over the side of the Mount of Olives. What a thrill it was to see the light breaking on Jerusalem— the walls of the city, the high places first. It touched David's tomb on Mount Zion, then touched the tops of the buildings, and then moved to the temple area. It was thrilling, and it was a picture of another bridegroom, the Lord Jesus Christ, the Sun of Righteousness. Some day He is coming in glory to this earth, but before He comes, He is going to take His church out of the world. He is the Bright and Morning Star. The Bright and Morning Star always appears before the sun rises. What a picture we have here in creation! There is nothing quite like it. This wonderful, wonderful psalm pictures creation.

GOD IN HIS COMMANDMENTS

The law of the LORD is perfect, converting the soul: the testimony of the LORD is sure, making wise the simple.

The statutes of the LORD are right, rejoicing the heart: the commandment of the LORD is pure, enlightening the eyes.

The fear of the LORD is clean, enduring for ever: the judgments of the LORD are true and righteous altogether.

More to be desired are they than gold, yea, than much fine gold: sweeter also than honey and the honeycomb.

Moreover by them is thy servant warned: and in keeping of them there is great reward [Ps. 19:7–11].

Again let me give you Dr. Gaebelein's translation: "The Law of Jehovah is perfect, restoring the soul; the testimony of Jehovah is sure, making wise the simple. The precepts of Jehovah are right, rejoicing the heart; the commandment of Jehovah is pure, enlightening the eyes; the fear of Jehovah is clean, enduring for ever; the judgments of Jehovah are truth, they are altogether righteous. More to be desired than gold, than much fine gold, and sweeter than honey, and honeycomb. By them thy servant is warned, in keeping them the reward is great" (*The Book of Psalms*, p. 91).

Now notice what he says about the commandments:

1. They are *perfect*. The Law cannot save us because it is perfect

and we are not. We cannot measure up to it, but there is nothing wrong with the Law. Paul, who set forth the grace of God, says this about the Law, "Wherefore the law is holy, and the commandment holy, and just, and good. Was then that which is good made death unto me? God forbid. But sin, that it might appear sin, working death in me by that which is good; that sin by the commandment might become exceeding sinful. For we know that the law is spiritual: but I am carnal, sold under sin" (Rom. 7:12–14). There is nothing *wrong* with the Law, but it is an administration of death to us because there is something radically wrong with us. The Law was given to show us that we are sinners before God. The Law is perfect.

2. "The testimony of the LORD is *sure.*" Don't bank on God changing to the "new" morality. God is not reading some of the new views of psychology, and He is not listening to the decisions that some judges are handing down. God is going to punish sin—He *says* that is what He is going to do. The testimony of the Lord is *sure.* Judgment is coming. The commandments reveal that.

3. "The statutes of the LORD are *right.*" Someone says, "There are certain commandments I don't like." Well, maybe you don't like them, but God does. They are right. What makes them right? In a college sociology class years ago, I had a professor who was always saying, "Who is going to determine what is right? How do you know what is right?" I didn't know the answer then, but now I know that God determines what is right. This is His universe; He made it, and He made the rules. Maybe you do not like the law of gravitation, but I advise you not to fool with it. That is, if you go to the top of a ten-story building, don't step off, because God will not suspend the law of gravitation for you. It operates for everyone, doesn't it?

4. "The commandment of the LORD is *pure.*" I tell you, it is pure. It will do something for you—ennoble you and lift you up.

5. "The fear of the LORD is *clean.*" We are told that this word *fear* means "reverential trust." I believe it means more than that. It means *fear.* We do well to fear God, my friend. I loved my Dad, but I sure was afraid of him. He kept me in line, and I think, in the final analysis, that is what kept me out of jail. I knew that when I did wrong there

would be trouble. The fear of the Lord is clean; the fear of the Lord will clean you up. Fear of my Dad made me a better boy, but I still loved him.

6. "The judgments of the LORD are true." Do you want to know what truth is? Pilate wanted to know. He asked our Lord, ". . . What is truth? . . ." (John 18:38), and Truth was standing right in front of him in the person of the Lord Jesus Christ.

7. "The judgments of the LORD are . . . righteous." They are right. Whatever God does is right. This is a tremendous section. We ought to learn to love all of the Word of God—all of it. Several people have written to me because they think I am opposed to the Ten Commandments. Why, the Ten Commandments are wonderful; I am not opposed to them. I am opposed to Vernon McGee—he can't keep them. If you can keep them, then you can ask God to move over; and you can sit beside Him because you have made it on your own. But God says you cannot keep them, and I agree with Him. He told me I would not make it on my own, and I agree with Him. I have to come as a sinner to God.

THE GRACE OF GOD IN CHRIST

This brings us to the grace of God in Christ.

> Who can understand his errors? cleanse thou me from secret faults.

> Keep back thy servant also from presumptuous sins; let them not have dominion over me: then shall I be upright, and I shall be innocent from the great transgression.

> Let the words of my mouth, and the meditation of my heart, be acceptable in thy sight, O LORD, my strength, and my redeemer [Ps. 19:12–14].

"Who can understand his errors?" Who can? I use subterfuge a great deal. My wife says I rationalize. In fact, I am pretty good at that. I can give excuses, but God won't accept them. God says that you cannot understand your errors. Just take His word for it that you are a sinner.

"Cleanse thou me from secret faults." Secret faults are the problem with a great many folk today. They are secret from themselves—they think they are not sinners.

"Keep back thy servant also from presumptuous sins . . . and I shall be innocent from the great transgression." Do you know what "the great transgression" is? It is the rejection of Jesus Christ, the One who is set before us in this psalm.

Now listen to the psalmist. This is a verse that you hear many times in a believer's prayer. "Let the words of my mouth, and the meditation of my heart, be acceptable in thy sight, O LORD, my strength, and my redeemer." Who was David's *strength*? Christ! Who was his redeemer? Christ. He is also my strength and my redeemer. He becomes that through the grace of God. What a wonderful psalm this is!

PSALM 20

THEME: Plea of Israel for the success of the Messiah

This psalm is not classed as one of the messianic psalms, but I have labeled it such because it is a prophecy of the Messiah and His work of redemption. I think it is closely linked with the two psalms that follow it. In Israel these psalms were sung together in a liturgical way. Some scholars think they were chanted by the leaders of worship, the Levites, and by the assembled worshipers who responded antiphonally.

Bishop Horne said, concerning this prayer psalm: "The Church prayeth for the prosperity of the King Messiah, going forth to battle, as her champion and deliverer; for His acceptance by the Father, and for the accomplishment of His will" (quoted in A. C. Gaebelein, *The Book of Psalms*, pp. 93–94). Bishop Horne would have hit the nail right on the head if he had said "the remnant of Israel" instead of "church." This psalm really deals with Israel.

This is another psalm that tells out the grace of God.

The Lord hear thee in the day of trouble; the name of the God of Jacob defend thee [Ps. 20:1].

"The day of trouble" is when we want Him to hear us, isn't it?

This is a psalm of David. How did old Jacob get in here? By the grace of God. God never was ashamed to be called the God of Jacob. I would have been ashamed of Jacob because of some of the things he did. Maybe you have been ashamed of him, too, but God was not. God saved Jacob by His grace.

Send thee help from the sanctuary, and strengthen thee out of Zion [Ps. 20:2].

What sanctuary is this verse talking about? The church? No! The sanctuary in Jerusalem. Where is Zion? Maybe you are thinking of Zion, Illinois, or Zion, Utah; but David is not talking about those places—nor any church. Zion is in Israel, of course. Nothing could be clearer.

Remember all thy offerings, and accept thy burnt sacrifice; Selah [Ps. 20:3].

Dr. Gaebelein translates it like this: "He shall remember all Thine offerings, and accept Thy burnt offerings. Selah." Notice that he is not referring to our offerings, but to Christ's offering. He offered up in the days of His flesh, not only prayers and tears (Heb. 5), but finally His own body.

"Selah"—here is something for you to meditate on, to think about, in these days when there is so much trouble.

Grant thee according to thine own heart, and fulfil all thy counsel.

We will rejoice in thy salvation, and in the name of our God we will set up our banners: the LORD fulfil all thy petitions.

Now know I that the LORD saveth his anointed; he will hear him from his holy heaven with the saving strength of his right hand [Ps. 20:4-6].

The Father is going to hear the prayers of the Lord Jesus. Remember that He said, ". . . Father, I thank thee that thou hast heard me. And I knew that thou hearest me always . . ." (John 11:41–42). Christ is probably the only One whom the Father always hears and always answers.

Some trust in chariots, and some in horses: but we will remember the name of the LORD our God.

> **They are brought down and fallen: but we are risen, and stand upright.**
>
> **Save, LORD: let the king hear us when we call [Ps. 20:7–9].**

The "king" is for Israel. For us today He is Savior, and we pray in the name of Jesus.

"Save, LORD" is *Hosanna* in the Hebrew. This is a great Hosanna psalm. May God make it real to our hearts.

PSALM 21

THEME: The ascension of Christ

This is another psalm which I consider messianic, although it is not on the list of messianic psalms that I gave in the introduction, nor is it quoted verbatim in the New Testament as referring to Christ. However, I don't think you can read it without coming to the judgment that it has reference to Him. In fact, Israel from the beginning said this psalm spoke of the Messiah. The Targum, which is the Chaldean paraphrase of the Old Testament, and the Talmud teach that the king mentioned in this psalm is the Messiah. The great Talmud scholar, Rabbi Solomon Isaaci, known as Rashi, born in A.D. 1040, endorsed this interpretation but suggested that it should be given up because of Christians making use of this psalm as an evidence that Jesus of Nazareth is the Messiah. I feel that this is a very good testimony to the fact that this psalm does refer to the Lord Jesus.

It is interesting to note that this psalm is used by the liturgical churches that observe certain days such as Ascension Day. They use this psalm as commemorating the Ascension, that is, the return of the Lord Jesus to glory and His presence there as our Great High Priest. I don't know why those of us who are fundamental in the faith have paid so little attention to the ascension of Christ. We observe Christmas and Easter and the Day of Pentecost, but we forget the ascension of Christ. To me that is a great day. Well, this psalm gives us the opportunity to give some thought to our Lord's ascension. We will see Him as king in heaven, and we will see the judgment that is to come upon those who have rejected Him.

This is another psalm of David, according to the inspired text, and includes Christ's coming reign as king on the earth. This psalm was undoubtedly used in temple worship. Dr. J. J. Stewart Perowne has made this comment: "Each Jewish Monarch was but a feeble type of Israel's true King: and all the hopes and aspirations of pious hearts, however, they might have for their immediate object the then reigning Monarch, whether David himself or one of his sons, still looked beyond these to Him, who should be David's Lord as well as his son" (*The Book of Psalms*, p. 207). That is quite a testimony coming from a man who was liberal in his theology.

Now notice how this psalm opens.

The king shall joy in thy strength, O LORD; and in thy salvation how greatly shall he rejoice! [Ps. 21:1].

Although David is speaking of his personal experience, the primary interpretation refers to the Lord Jesus Christ.

"The king shall joy in thy strength." In Hebrews 12:2 it was said of the Lord, ". . . who for the joy that was set before him endured the cross, despising the shame,"—and He ascended into heaven—"and is set down at the right hand of the throne of God." This verse speaks of the joy of our Lord in having wrought our salvation for us. He rejoices in the power and strength that have been bestowed upon Him. He has gone to heaven, and the angels and principalities have been made subject to Him. Today He is able to save to the uttermost those who come to God through Him (Heb. 7:25). This is a wonderful psalm.

Thou hast given him his heart's desire, and hast not withholden the request of his lips. Selah [Ps. 21:2].

When the Lord made His final report to His Father in His High Priestly prayer in John 17, He said, ". . . Father, the hour is come; glorify thy Son, that thy Son also may glorify thee" (John 17:1). This prayer, and all of the Lord's other requests, have been and will be answered, as we see in this prayer. This is the prayer of ascension. He is at God's right hand. "Thou hast given him his heart's desire." When He was here on earth, the Lord could say, "Father, I will that they also, whom thou hast given me, be with me where I am; that they may behold my glory, which thou hast given me: for thou lovedst me before the foundation of the world" (John 17:24). This prayer will be answered in the future when we are with Him. He came to earth to make this possible. The Father has not withheld the request of His Son's lips. "Selah"—this is something we ought to meditate about.

> He asked life of thee, and thou gavest it him, even length of days for ever and ever.
>
> His glory is great in thy salvation: honour and majesty hast thou laid upon him.
>
> For thou hast made him most blessed for ever: thou hast made him exceeding glad with thy countenance [Ps. 21:4–6].

Now notice Dr. Gaebelein's translation of these verses: "He asked life of Thee, Thou gavest it Him: length of days for ever and ever. His glory is great in Thy salvation; Honour and majesty hast Thou laid upon Him. For Thou hast made Him most blessed for ever: Thou dost delight Him with joy in Thy presence" (The Book of Psalms, p. 98).

The Lord Jesus Christ came to give His life a ransom for many down here. On earth you find Him in humiliation, and you find Him pleading again and again in prayer. He agonized in the Garden of Gethsemane. Psalm 102:23–24 says of the Lord: "He weakened my strength in the way; he shortened my days. I said, O my God, take me not away in the midst of my days: thy years are throughout all generations." He asked for life. He died in the very prime of life. He was thirty-three years old. He prayed, ". . . Father, if thou be willing, remove this cup from me: nevertheless not my will, but thine, be done" (Luke 22:42). In Hebrews 5:7 we are told: "Who in the days of his flesh, when he had offered up prayers and supplications with strong crying and tears unto him that was able to save him from death, and was heard in that he feared." How was He heard? He died! But God raised Him from the dead. Now He lives in His glorified human body for ever and ever. He is now at God's right hand. "His glory is great in Thy salvation." Oh, the glory that should accrue to Him because He saved you, and He saved me!

> For the king trusteth in the LORD, and through the mercy
> of the most High he shall not be moved.
>
> Thine hand shall find out all thine enemies: thy right
> hand shall find out those that hate thee.
>
> Thou shalt make them as a fiery oven in the time of thine
> anger: the LORD shall swallow them up in his wrath, and
> the fire shall devour them [Ps. 21:7–9].

Dr. Gaebelein translates it: "Thy hand shall find out all Thine enemies; Thy right hand shall find out those that hate Thee. Thou shalt
make them as a fiery oven in the time of Thy coming" (*The Book of
Psalms*, p. 99). Not only is He a God of salvation but, because of His
death upon the cross for sinners, He is also a God of judgment. Those
who have rejected Him are His enemies. You don't believe in hell?
The Bible teaches it. If you don't believe there is a hell, you are in
disagreement with the Bible.

A man once came to me and said, "I don't believe in hell." I replied, "Do you know that you are in disagreement with the Bible?" He
said, "I don't care. I don't believe there is a hell." Well, I told him,
"You will someday. The day will come when you will find that it is
true." Hell is not a pleasant subject. Who said that it was? God does
not take any delight in the lost. God's judgment is called His strange
work. His wonderful work is salvation. He *wants* to save. If you won't
come to Him His way, or if you don't want His salvation, then there is
nothing but judgment that remains.

"Thou shalt make them as a fiery oven in the time of thine anger:
the LORD shall swallow them up in his wrath, and the fire shall devour
them." This verse is clear. Fire is fire, and judgment is judgment.

> Their fruit shalt thou destroy from the earth, and their
> seed from among the children of men.
>
> For they intended evil against thee: they imagined a
> mischievous device, which they are not able to perform.

Therefore shalt thou make them turn their back, when thou shalt make ready thine arrows upon thy strings against the face of them.

Be thou exalted, LORD, in thine own strength: so will we sing and praise thy power [Ps. 21:10–13].

In this marvelous psalm we see Christ's cross and suffering. He endured the cross ". . . for the *joy* that was set before him" (Heb. 12:2). His prayers have been answered. Now the King is in heaven. We see Him there crowned with glory and honor. He is there on behalf of His people. He is there in unspeakable joy and waiting for His manifestation and kingly glory.

I would like to give you another picture of the Lord Jesus Christ today. The first time He came to earth He was a man of sorrows and acquainted with grief. Somebody says, "Every picture I have ever seen of Him is a solemn, serious looking Christ." I don't care for the pictures that have been painted of Christ, and I know He doesn't look like that today. He is sitting at God's right hand, and His heart is filled with joy. He wants to communicate that joy to you and me. Oh, that we might get a glimpse of *Him* today! When the Lord was on earth, His enemies conspired against Him, but He trusted in Jehovah. In John's vision in Revelation 12 the dragon, representing Satan, wanted to devour the manchild, representing Christ. (The woman is Israel.) Before the dragon could devour the manchild, He was caught up to God and to His throne. That is where He is right now.

Also this psalm gives us a picture of judgment, which is amplified greatly in the Book of Revelation. That is a serious picture that is given to us there. Paul the apostle mentions it also in 2 Thessalonians 1:7–8: "And to you who are troubled, rest with us, when the Lord Jesus shall be revealed from heaven with his mighty angels, in flaming fire taking vengeance on them that know not God, and that obey not the gospel of our Lord Jesus Christ." This is a picture of the Lord's coming in judgment upon His enemies. 2 Thessalonians 1:9–10 goes on to say, "Who shall be punished with everlasting destruction from the presence of the Lord, and from the glory of his power; When he shall come to be glorified in his saints, and to be admired in all them that believe (because our testimony among you was believed) in that day."

This is a glorious psalm of the Ascension of Christ. What is your relationship to Him today? If He is not your Savior, if you have not trusted the One who came down here to die, then judgment is coming upon you someday. But today He is filled with joy up yonder at God's right hand, because He has wrought out your salvation and mine. This wonderful ascension psalm makes very clear the glorious grace of God in Christ Jesus.

PSALM 22

THEME: The crucifixion of Christ

There are several Scriptures with which I never feel adequate to deal. This is one of them. When we come to Psalm 22 I feel that we are standing on holy ground, and we should take off our spiritual shoes. This psalm is called the Psalm of the Cross. It is so named because it describes more accurately and minutely the crucifixion of Christ than does any other portion of the Word of God. It corresponds, of course, to the twenty-second chapter of Genesis and the fifty-third chapter of Isaiah.

We have many messianic psalms which are pictures of Christ. The first psalm, for instance, is a portrait of Christ in His character—who He is, His life, His practice. But in Psalm 22 we have an X-ray which penetrates into His thoughts and into His inner life. In this psalm we see the anguish of His passion; His soul is laid bare. In the Gospels is recorded the historical fact of His death, and some of the events which attended His crucifixion; but only in Psalm 22 are His thoughts revealed. It has been the belief of many scholars that actually the Lord Jesus, while on the cross, quoted the entire twenty-second psalm. I concur in this, because the seven last sayings that are given in the Gospels either appear in this psalm or the psychological background for them is here.

It is the custom in many churches to conduct a Good Friday service in which seven ministers bring messages from the seven last sayings of Christ from the cross. In the course of fifteen years, I have heard over one hundred men deal with these seven words. It is always a spiritual feast to hear how each man develops the subject, and always there are many new and profitable thoughts presented. However, we shall attempt to encompass all seven sayings in one message. And instead of standing beneath the cross and listening to Him, we are going to hang on the cross with Him. We shall view the crucifixion of

Christ from a new position—from the cross itself. And we can look with Him on those beneath His cross, as He was hanging there, and see what went on in His heart and in His mind. We shall see what occurred in His soul as He became the sacrifice for the sins of the world. As He was suspended there between heaven and earth, He became the ladder let down from heaven to this earth so that men might have a way to God.

We were there, if you please, on that cross as He was made sin for us—He ". . . who knew no sin; that we might be made the righteousness of God in him" (2 Cor. 5:21). We were as truly on that cross when He died as we today are in Christ by faith. Peter put it like this: "Who his own self bare our sins in his own body on the tree, that we, being dead to sins, should live unto righteousness: by whose stripes ye were healed" (1 Pet. 2:24). Healed from sin!

"MY GOD, MY GOD, WHY HAST THOU FORSAKEN ME?"

Psalm 22 opens with the plaintive and desperate cry of this poor, lone Man, forsaken of God.

> My God, my God, why hast thou forsaken me? why art thou so far from helping me, and from the words of my roaring? [Ps. 22:1].

There has been an attempt made to play down the stark reality and the bitter truth that He was forsaken of God. I hold an article written by a local minister who takes the position that Jesus was not forsaken. He attempts to translate, "Eli, Eli, lama sabachthani" to mean, "My God, my God, for this was I kept." His authority is the Peshitta, or the Syriac version. However, the Peshitta is not a good manuscript. It never has been used by any reputable translator, for it is not a good translation. Evidently it was made by some who had gone into a heresy at the very beginning. The value of it is that in many places it throws light on the customs in Palestine during that period. I have used it in that connection on several occasions, but never would I accept the translation. Actually, the Hebrew is very clear, and the Greek is very clear, and the

Aramaic is very clear—in each language the cry means that Jesus was forsaken of God.

Now we have here—and this is something I want to emphasize from the very beginning—a record of His *human suffering*. We see Him hanging there as a man, ". . . the Lamb of God, which taketh away the sin of the world" (John 1:29). We get more light on this by turning to the Epistle to the Hebrews: "But we see Jesus, who was made a little lower than the angels [a little lower than the angels? Yes, made a man. Why?] for the suffering of death, crowned with glory and honour; that he by the grace of God should taste death for every man" (Heb. 2:9). That is what we are looking at—the One who left heaven's glory and became a Man. He became a Man to reveal God, yes, that is true; but most of all to redeem man. "Forasmuch then as the children are partakers of flesh and blood, he also himself likewise took part of the same; that through death he might destroy him that had the power of death, that is, the devil" (Heb. 2:14).

He could save no one by His life; it was His sacrificial death that saves. "And deliver them who through fear of death were all their lifetime subject to bondage. For verily he took not on him the nature of angels; but he took on him the seed of Abraham. . . . For in that he himself hath suffered being tempted, he is able to succour them [help them] that are tempted" (Heb. 2:15–16, 18). We see the Man Christ Jesus on the cross as the perfect Man. He had learned to rest upon God. He had learned to trust Him in all that He did. He said, ". . . I do always those things that please him" (John 8:29). But yonder in that desperate and despairing hour He was abandoned of God. There was no place to turn, either on the human plane or on the divine. He had no place to go. The Man Christ Jesus was forsaken. No other ever has had to experience that. No one. He alone.

Why did God forsake Him?

But thou art holy, O thou that inhabitest the praises of Israel [Ps. 22:3].

Why was He forsaken of God? Because on the cross in those last three hours, in the impenetrable darkness, He was made sin.

> But none of the ransomed ever knew
> How deep were the waters crossed;
> Nor how dark was the night that the Lord
>   passed through
> Ere He found His sheep that was lost.

He was forsaken for a brief moment. The paradox is that at that very moment God was in Christ reconciling the world unto Himself. And the Lord Jesus Himself said, "Behold, the hour cometh, yea, is now come, that ye shall be scattered, every man to his own, and shall leave me alone: and yet I am not alone, because the Father is with me" (John 16:32). The Father was with Him when He was in prison, the Father was with Him when He was being beaten, the Father was with Him when they nailed Him to the cross. But in these last three hours He made His soul an offering for sin, and it pleased the Father to bruise Him (see Isa. 53:10).

Forsaken. My friend, you do not know what that is; and I do not know what it is to be forsaken of God. The vilest man on this earth today is not forsaken of God. Anyone can turn to Him. But when Christ takes my sin upon Himself, He is forsaken of God.

"Why hast thou forsaken me?" It is not the *why* of impatience. It is not the *why* of despair; it is not the *why* of doubt. It is the human cry of intense suffering, aggravated by the anguish of His innocent and holy life. That awful and agonizing cry of the loneliness of His passion! He was alone. He was alone with the sins of the world upon Him.

"Why art thou so far from helping me, and from the words of my roaring?" (Ps. 22:1). Roaring? Yes. At His trial He was silent, ". . . as a sheep before her shearers is dumb, so he openeth not his mouth" (Isa. 53:7). When they beat Him, He said nothing; when they nailed Him to the cross, He did not whimper. But when God forsook Him, He roared like a lion. It was a roar of pain. Have you ever been in the woods when dogs attacked an animal? Have you heard the shriek of that animal? There is nothing quite like it. And that is what the writer is attempting to convey to us here. I think that shriek from the cross rent the rocks, for it had been His voice that had created them. Now the Creator is suffering! On that cross He cried like a wounded animal; His was not even a human cry, but like a wild, roaring lion. It was the plaintive shriek and the wail of unutterable woe as our sins were pressed down upon Him.

But I am a worm, and no man; a reproach of men, and despised of the people [Ps. 22:6].

What does He mean when He says, "I am a worm"? He has roared like a lion; now He says, "I am a worm." It is because He has reached the very lowest place. "He is despised and rejected of men; a man of sorrows, and acquainted with grief: and we hid as it were our faces from him; he was despised, and we esteemed him not" (Isa. 53:3). "I am a worm." The interesting thing is that the word used here for worm means the coccus worm, which was used by the Hebrews in dyeing all the curtains of the tabernacle scarlet red. When He said, "I am a worm," He meant more than that He had reached the lowest level. It was He who had said, ". . . though your sins be as scarlet, they shall be as white as snow . . ." (Isa. 1:18). Only His blood, my friend, can rub out that dark, deep spot in your life.

Lady Macbeth, sleepwalking that night, went up and down rubbing her hands, insane with the guilt of murder. She says, "All the perfumes of Arabia will not sweeten this little hand." And she was right; they could not. She seemed to be continually washing her hands as she rubbed them together, and she cried, "Out damned spot! out, I say!" (*Macbeth*, Act V, Scene 1).

My friend, there is only one thing that will take the spot of sin out of your life, that is the blood of Christ. The blood of the Lord Jesus, God's Son, cleanses from all sin. Only His blood.

"FATHER, FORGIVE THEM"

Will you look at that victim on the cross? His suffering is intensified by that brutal mob and hardened spectators that are beneath Him. Look through His eyes and see what He sees.

All they that see me laugh me to scorn: they shoot out the lip, they shake the head, saying,

> He trusted on the LORD that he would deliver him: let him deliver him, seeing he delighted in him [Ps. 22:7–8].

Some criminals have been so detested that they have been taken from jail and lynched by a mob. But while the criminal was being executed, the mob would disperse. Tempers were cooled, and emotions were assuaged. But not this crowd! I think the lowest thing that ever has been said of religion was said of these Pharisees when the Lord Jesus Christ was dying: "And sitting down they watched him there" (Matt. 27:36). You have to be low to do that. In fact, you cannot get lower than that! The venom and vileness of the human heart were being poured out like an open sewer as they remained there and ridiculed Him in His death. After a snake has put its deadly fangs into its victim and emitted its poison, it will slither away in the grass. But not this crowd—not the human heart in rebellion against God.

"Then said Jesus, Father, forgive them: for they know not what they do . . ." (Luke 23:34). If He had not said that, this crowd would have committed the unpardonable sin. But they did not—He asked forgiveness for their sin. We know that the centurion in charge of the execution was saved; and a whole company of Pharisees, including Saul of Tarsus, who probably was in this crowd, were saved.

"WOMAN, BEHOLD THY SON!"

Now as He looks over the crowd He sees not only eyes of hate and antagonism, but He sees eyes of love. He sees His mother with John down there. "Now there stood by the cross of Jesus his mother . . ." (John 19:25). As Jesus looks at her, do you want to know what went on in His heart? He went back to Bethlehem at the time He was born, and He says to the Father:

> But thou art he that took me out of the womb: thou didst make me hope when I was upon my mother's breasts.
>
> I was cast upon thee from the womb: thou art my God from my mother's belly [Ps. 22:9–10].

". . . Woman, behold thy son!" (John 19:26). Yonder at the wedding at Cana in Galilee, she had asked Him to do something to show that He was the Messiah, that she was right when she said He was virgin born. She wanted Him to reveal Himself at this wedding. His answer to her at that time was, ". . . Woman, what have I to do with thee? mine hour is not yet come" (John 2:4). But there hanging on the cross: ". . . Woman, behold thy son!" His hour has come! The reason for His coming into the world is now being accomplished. This is the most important hour in the history of the world!

Then His attention moves back to those who are doing the crucifying.

Many bulls have compassed me: strong bulls of Bashan have beset me round [Ps. 22:12].

Describing these soldiers that were crucifying Him, He says they are like the bulls of Bashan; but He does not stop with that, for He is being devoured by wild animals—that is what His tormentors had become:

They gaped upon me with their mouths, as a ravening and a roaring lion [Ps. 22:13].

He is talking about Rome now—Rome crucified Him. He compares them to a roaring lion, for the lion was the picture of Rome.

Now notice His condition:

I am poured out like water, and all my bones are out of joint: my heart is like wax; it is melted in the midst of my bowels [Ps. 22:14].

This accurate description of crucifixion is remarkable when you consider that crucifixion was unknown when this psalm was written. The Roman Empire was not even in existence, and it was Rome that instituted crucifixion. Yet here is a picture of a man dying by crucifixion!

"I am poured out like water"—the excessive perspiration of a dying man out in that sun.

"All my bones are out of joint"—the horrible thing about crucifixion is that when a man began to lose blood, his strength ebbed from him, and all his bones slipped out of joint. That is an awful thing. It was terrible, terrible suffering.

Then He says something that is indeed strange, "My heart is like wax." He died of a broken heart. Many doctors have said that a ruptured heart would have produced what John meticulously recorded. "But one of the soldiers with a spear pierced his side, and forthwith came there out blood and water" (John 19:34). Let me paraphrase that. "I saw that Roman soldier put the spear in His side and there came out blood and water—not just blood but blood and water." John took note of that and recorded it. May I say to you, Jesus died of a broken heart.

"I THIRST"

As He is hanging there ready to expire, with excessive perspiration pouring from Him, He suffers the agony of thirst.

> **My strength is dried up like a potsherd; and my tongue cleaveth to my jaws; and thou hast brought me into the dust of death [Ps. 22:15].**

Down beneath the cross they hear Him say, "I thirst."

> **For dogs have compassed me: the assembly of the wicked have enclosed me: they pierced my hands and my feet [Ps. 22:16].**

"Dog" was the name for Gentiles. The piercing of His hands and feet is an accurate description of crucifixion.

> **I may tell all my bones: they look and stare upon me.**

> **They part my garments among them, and cast lots upon my vesture [Ps. 22:17–18].**

He was crucified naked. It is difficult for us in this age of nudity and pornography to comprehend the great humiliation He suffered by hanging nude on the cross. They had taken his garments and gambled for ownership. My friend, He went through it all, crucified naked, that you might be clothed with the righteousness of Christ, and so be able to stand before God throughout the endless ages of eternity.

"FATHER, INTO THY HANDS
I COMMEND MY SPIRIT"

But be not thou far from me, O LORD: O my strength, haste thee to help me.

Deliver my soul from the sword; my darling from the power of the dog [Ps. 22:19–20].

The word *darling* is better translated "my only one"—"This is my beloved Son . . ." (Matt. 3:17). "Deliver my soul from the sword; my *only* one from the power of the dog." Jesus is saying, ". . . Father, into thy hands I commend my spirit . . ." (Luke 23:46).

Save me from the lion's mouth: for thou hast heard me from the horns of the unicorns [Ps. 22:21].

One of the most remarkable statements is this: "thou hast heard me from the horns of the unicorns." To express intensity in the Hebrew, the plural is used—horns of the unicorns; but the thought is *one horn*.

For many years it was thought that the unicorn was a mythical animal, but recent investigation has revealed that it was an animal a size smaller than the elephant, very much like the rhinoceros, sometimes called a wild bull. Vicious and brutal, every one of them was a killer. And the thing that identified them was the fact that they had *one horn*. "Thou hast heard me from the horns of the unicorns"—*uni* means "one"—one horn. To me, my beloved, that is remarkable indeed; because the cross on which the Lord Jesus Christ was crucified was probably not the shaped cross that we see today. We think of a cross made of an upright with a crosspiece. Nowhere does Scripture so describe it.

There are two Greek words that are translated by the English word *cross*. One of them is the word *stauros*. You find it used in several places. For instance: ". . . Thou that destroyest the temple, and buildest it in three days, save thyself. If thou be the Son of God, come down from the cross" (Matt. 27:40). The word *cross* is *stauros*, meaning "one piece." It is interesting how accurate Scripture is, but how tradition has been woven into it in our thinking. Paul used the word *stauros* when he wrote: "For the preaching of the cross [*stauros*] is to them that perish foolishness; but unto us which are saved it is the power of God" (1 Cor. 1:18).

The second Greek word is *xulon*, which is translated by the English "cross" or "tree." It simply means a piece of wood. Paul also used this word: "And when they had fulfilled all that was written of him, they took him down from the tree [*xulon*], and laid him in a sepulchre" (Acts 13:29).

They took Him down from the tree! Does he mean an upright with a crosspiece? Now I am perfectly willing to go along with the popularly accepted shape of a cross, but for the sake of accuracy and to appreciate the exactness of this psalm, we need to brush aside tradition for a moment. Jesus said, "thou hast heard me from the horns of the unicorns [the cross]." ". . . Into thy hands I commend my spirit . . ." (Luke 23:46).

Another thing that amazes me is that this word *xulon*, translated "tree" or "cross," is mentioned in the twenty-second chapter of Revelation as the tree of life! I believe that the tree on which Jesus died will be there, alive, throughout the endless ages of eternity, to let you and me know what it cost to redeem us.

Now when we come to verse 22 of this psalm, we see a radical change, a bifurcation. We have had the sufferings of Christ described for us; now we see the glory that should follow.

I will declare thy name unto my brethren: in the midst of the congregation will I praise thee [Ps. 22:22].

I think that He said this entire psalm on the cross. He did not die defeated; for when He reached the very end He said, "This is the gospel that will be witnessed to. I will declare thy name unto my brethren." And I see Peter in the midst of the Sanhedrin, composed of both Pharisees and Sadducees, saying to them, ". . . there is none other name under heaven given among men, whereby we must be saved" (Acts 4:12). "I will declare thy name unto my brethren."

"TODAY SHALT THOU BE WITH ME IN PARADISE"

My praise shall be of thee in the great congregation: I will pay my vows before them that fear him.

The meek shall eat and be satisfied: they shall praise the LORD that seek him: your heart shall live for ever [Ps. 22:25–26].

The thief on the cross said, ". . . Lord, remember me when thou comest into thy kingdom" (Luke 23:42). Christ says, "I'll pay my vows"—". . . Today shalt thou be with me in paradise" (Luke 23:43). The redeemed shall be there to praise, and the thief He was taking with Him that very day. Although he was a man unfit to even live down here, according to Rome's standard, the Lord Jesus makes him fit for heaven by His death on the cross.

"IT IS FINISHED"

There is a seventh word; it is His last.

They shall come, and shall declare his righteousness unto a people that shall be born, that he hath done this [Ps. 22:31].

"To a people that shall be born" includes you, my friend.

They shall declare *His* righteousness—not your righteousness, for God says it is filthy rags in His sight. How will they declare His righteousness? "That he hath done this." Some would translate it, "It is finished," the last word He spoke on the cross. And when He said it, it was but one word—*Tetelestai!* Finished! Your redemption is a complete package, and He presents it to you wrapped up with everything in it. He doesn't want you to bring your do-it-yourself kit along. He does not need that. When He died on the cross, He provided a righteousness that would satisfy a holy God. All He asks of you is that you receive this package, this gift of God, which is eternal life in Christ Jesus.

If you reject it, God must treat you as He treated His Son when He cried, ". . . My God, my God, why hast thou forsaken me?" (Mark 15:34). I am not here to argue about the temperature of hell: it will be hell for any man to be forsaken of God. Jesus Christ went through it that you might never have to utter that cry.

Psalm 22 reveals the heart of our Savior as He was made a sin offering in our behalf. He completed the transaction in triumph. He offers to us a finished redemption. We never shall be worthy of it; we cannot earn it; we cannot buy it—we must receive it as a gift. Over nineteen hundred years ago the Lord Jesus Christ did all that was needed to save us.

It is done. *Tetelestai.* Finished!

PSALM 23

Psalm 23, which is so popular, would be meaningless without Psalm 22, which leads me to say that we have a trilogy or triptych of psalms that belong together. They are Psalms 22, 23, and 24, and they are called the shepherd psalms. These three psalms present the following picture of our Lord: In Psalm 22 He is the Good Shepherd. The Lord Jesus Himself made the statement, "I am the good shepherd: the good shepherd giveth his life for the sheep" (John 10:11). Now here in Psalm 23 He is the Great Shepherd. Notice this title in the great benediction at the conclusion of the Epistle to the Hebrews: "Now the God of peace, that brought again from the dead our Lord Jesus, that great shepherd of the sheep, through the blood of the everlasting covenant, Make you perfect in every good work to do his will, working in you that which is well-pleasing in his sight, through Jesus Christ; to whom be glory for ever and ever. Amen" (Heb. 13:20–21). Psalm 23 reveals Him as the Great Shepherd. Next, we see Him in Psalm 24 as the Chief Shepherd. "And when the chief Shepherd shall appear, ye shall receive a crown of glory that fadeth not away" (1 Pet. 5:4).

To put it succinctly, in Psalm 22 we see the *cross,* in Psalm 23 the *crook* (the Shepherd's crook), and in Psalm 24 the *crown* (the King's crown). In Psalm 22 Christ is the *Savior;* in Psalm 23 He is the *Satisfier;* in Psalm 24 He is the *Sovereign.* In Psalm 22 He is the *foundation;* in Psalm 23 He is the *manifestation;* in Psalm 24 He is the *expectation.* In Psalm 22 He *dies;* in Psalm 23 He is *living;* in Psalm 24 He is *coming.* Psalm 22 speaks of the *past;* Psalm 23 speaks of the *present;* and Psalm 24 speaks of the *future.* In Psalm 22 He gives His *life* for the sheep; in Psalm 23 He gives His *love* to the sheep; in Psalm 24 He gives us *light* when He shall appear. What a wonderful picture we have of Christ in these three psalms!

Now let us zero in on Psalm 23, probably the most familiar passage there is in the Word of God. No portion in writing of any time or of any work has been so widely circulated. Jews, both Orthodox and Reformed, know this psalm. Christians of all denominations are acquainted with this psalm. The world has caught its beauty.

Much has been written about this psalm, although its six verses are short and simple. It is like the Gettysburg Address as far as brevity is concerned. Someone has said, "I do not care how much a man says, if he says it in a few words." Someone else has said, "If folk who do not have anything to say would refrain from saying it, it would be a better world." Psalm 23 has few words. There was a business executive years ago who had a little motto on the wall of his office for all to see. It said, If you have anything important to say, say it in five minutes. Well, it only takes about forty-five seconds to read Psalm 23. It is brief. It is not the language of philosophy. It is not the language of theology. It is not a legal or scientific document. It is sublimely simple and simply sublime.

Before we look at the text itself, there are some things we should consider about this psalm. It is agreed that David is the author, but the question has always been: Did he write it when he was a shepherd boy or when he was an aged king? It is important to know the answer. Dr. Frank Morgan has called this "The Song of the Old Shepherd." I like that, and I agree with him. David the king never forgot David the shepherd boy. In Psalm 23 you do not have the musings of a green, inexperienced lad but the mature deliberations of a ripe experience. You see, David, when he came close to the end of his life, looked back upon his checkered career. It was then that he wrote this psalm. The old king on the throne remembered the shepherd boy. Life had beaten, battered, baffled, and bludgeoned this man. He was a hardened soldier, a veteran who knew victory, privation, hardship. He knew song and shadow. He was tested and tried. Therefore in Psalm 23 we do not have the theorizing of immaturity but fruit and the mature judgment born of a long life.

This psalm begins by saying, "The Lord is my shepherd." By what authority do you say my shepherd? Is this psalm for everybody? I don't think so. Since Psalms 22, 23, and 24 go together and tell one story, you have to know the Lord Jesus Christ as the Good Shepherd who gave His life for the sheep before you can know Him as the Great Shepherd. You must know the Shepherd of Psalm 22 before you can come to Psalm 23 and say, "The LORD is my shepherd."

REVELATION OF THE SANCTUARY
OF THE SHEPHERD'S SOUL

The LORD is my shepherd; I shall not want.

He maketh me to lie down in green pastures: he leadeth me beside the still waters [Ps. 23:1–2].

Notice "my shepherd . . . I shall not want . . . He maketh me to lie down . . . he leadeth me." This is a "he and me" psalm. The emphasis is upon the fact that there is nothing between the man's soul and God. "The LORD is my shepherd."

Verse 1 is a declaration and a deduction. It is one thing to say, "The Lord is a shepherd"—many people say that, and it sounds good. But can you make it personal and say, "The LORD is my shepherd"? By the authority of His redemptive work, His death and resurrection, you can trust Him and call Him your shepherd. It is also easy to say, "The Lord will be my shepherd," but David did not say that either. He said, "The LORD is my shepherd." This is his declaration.

"I shall not want"—notice that David does not say, I have not wanted, but "I shall not want." What is it that I need? Well, I need safety. I'm a sheep, a stupid little animal. Therefore, my Shepherd sees to it that I won't want for protection. He protects me. When a little sheep says, "I shall not want" and "I shall never perish," it is because it has a wonderful Shepherd. "I shall not want" looks into the future and gives assurance to the child of God. The security of the believer rests upon the Shepherd. And the believer's deduction rests upon his declaration.

A friend of mine who moved to Oregon once heard me talk about sheep. He said to me later, "Dr. McGee, you gave me the impression that sheep are nice, sweet little animals. You made them appear so helpless. I want to show you some sheep." He invited me to dinner. He gathered several sheep together, and after dinner we went out to look at them. As we watched them, he told me, "These sheep are stubborn, hardheaded, and pigheaded animals. Besides that, they are dirty and filthy." I said, "That's a picture of the human race." They do set us forth!

Not only do sheep need safety, they need sufficiency and satisfaction. "He maketh me to lie down in green pastures." That is sufficiency. Folk that know sheep tell us that a hungry sheep will not lie down. When sheep are lying down in green pastures, it means they have their tummies full. And Christ is our sufficiency. "And Jesus said unto them, I am the bread of life: he that cometh to me shall never hunger; and he that believeth on me shall never thirst" (John 6:35).

"He leadeth me beside the still waters." Sheep are frightened by turbulent water. And they don't like stagnant water. They don't want to drink where the hogs drink. All of this applies to the human family. We need rest in our day—not so much physical or mental rest, but rest of the soul. Remember what David said in Psalm 55:6: "Oh that I had wings like a dove! for then would I fly away, and be at rest." He wanted to get away from it all. But he found out that getting away from it all did not solve his problems. He had to learn to put his trust in the Lord, rest in Him, and wait patiently upon Him. The Lord Jesus says, "Come unto me, all ye that labour and are heavy laden, and I will rest you" (Matt. 11:28).

RECORD OF THE THOUGHTS
OF THE SHEPHERD'S MIND

He restoreth my soul: he leadeth me in the paths of righteousness for his name's sake.

Yea, though I walk through the valley of the shadow of death, I will fear no evil: for thou art with me; thy rod and thy staff they comfort me [Ps. 23:3–4].

"He restoreth my soul." David knew what that was. David had sinned—he was that little lost sheep that had strayed from the fold, and his Shepherd had restored him.

"He leadeth me in the paths of righteousness for his name's sake."
He leads, but we must follow. The Lord Jesus said to the religious
rulers who were actually His enemies, ". . . I told you, and ye believed
not: the works that I do in my Father's name, they bear witness of me.
But ye believe not, because ye are not of my sheep, as I said unto you.
My sheep hear my voice, and I know them, and they follow me" (John
10:25–27). Sheep will follow their own shepherd. That is the way you
can tell the one to whom the sheep belong. In Jesus' day the shepherd
never drove his sheep; he led them. That is no longer the case. When I
visited the land of Israel, I very seldom saw a shepherd walking ahead
of his sheep. But in the time of Christ, the shepherd was with his
sheep day after day. They knew him and they followed him. Our Shepherd leads us in right paths, and it is up to us to follow Him.

"Yea, though I walk through the valley of the shadow of death, I
will fear no evil." Here is courage and comfort. Death is the supreme
test of life. This is not just talking about the deathbed. Our human
family lives in the shadow of death. When a person is born, he starts
down a great canyon, and that canyon is the valley of the shadow of
death. You are in it constantly. In Los Angeles they say that when you
cross the street, you better move in a hurry because we have only the
quick and the dead. If you are not quick, you will be dead. All of us
walk in the shadow of death. As someone has said, the moment that
gives you life begins to take it away from you. All of us are in death's
valley. The shadow of death is on us. But, all the while I walk through
that valley, I will fear no evil. This is the encouraging comfort He
gives. If one of our loved ones dies as a child of God, this is our courage and comfort.

"I will fear no evil: for thou art with me." We can know that our
Shepherd is with us at all times, and even at the time of death. And I
want Him *with* me when my time comes to die.

"Thy rod and thy staff they comfort me." A rod was for defense,
and a staff was for direction. He gives us gentle reproof and severe
rebuke. He has a rod for our defense, but He also has a staff for our
direction. He has a staff for the little old sheep that are bound to stray.
That comforts me. Now that I am getting to be an old man, I look back
on my life and I realize that indeed that rod is a comfort. He used it on

me several times, and I thank Him for it because it got me back into the fold. We all need that.

REFLECTION OF THE HAPPINESS AND HOPE
OF THE SHEPHERD'S HEART

Thou preparest a table before me in the presence of mine enemies: thou anointest my head with oil; my cup runneth over.

Surely goodness and mercy shall follow me all the days of my life: and I will dwell in the house of the LORD for ever [Ps. 23:5–6].

These two verses reflect the happiness and hope of the Shepherd's heart. "Thou preparest a table before me in the presence of mine enemies." Here we have felicity, fruitfulness, and fullness. All of that is undergirded with joy. What is that table today? I think it speaks of the Lord's table. At the time this psalm was written it spoke of God's promise to Israel of physical blessings; to us He promises spiritual blessings.

"Thou anointest my head with oil." That oil speaks of the Holy Spirit. We need that anointing today. We cannot face life alone.

"My cup runneth over." This is symbolic of joy. We need to be undergirded with joy today. The Lord says, ". . . I am come that they might have life, and that they might have it more abundantly" (John 10:10). The Lord wants our joy to be full. It reminds me of the little girl who said, "Lord, fill up my cup. I can't hold very much, but I can run over a whole lot." Oh, how this world needs Christians who are running over!

This brings us to the final verse of this psalm. Our Shepherd brings us all the way from the green pastures and the still waters to the Father's house. "Surely goodness and mercy shall follow me all the days of my life: and I will dwell in the house of the LORD for ever." In John 14:2–3 the Lord says to us, ". . . I go to prepare a place for you. And if I go and prepare a place for you, I will come again, and receive you unto myself; that where I am, there ye may be also." You know, we are not pedigreed sheep, and sheep are not worth much anyway, but we do have a wonderful Shepherd. Can you say at this moment, "The LORD is my shepherd"? If you can, all the wonderful promises of this psalm are yours. If He is the Shepherd who gave His life for the sheep and He is your Savior, this psalm is for you.

PSALM 24

This is the psalm of the crown. It speaks of the coming of the Chief Shepherd. Tradition says it was composed by David and sung when he brought up the ark from Kirjath-jearim to Mount Zion (1 Chronicles 13:1–8). It was sung in an antiphonal way. It has been suggested that it was sung by the chorus of the procession and by solo voices. Josephus, the Jewish historian, says that seven choirs of singers and musicians marched before the ark as it was brought to Mount Zion where David had prepared a tabernacle for it until the temple was built. I think it will help us to appreciate the thrill of this psalm if we use the possible arrangement as suggested by Delitzsch and Gaebelein.

The psalm divides itself into two sections: the companions of the King who enter the kingdom (vv. 1–6), and the coming of the King to set up the kingdom (vv. 7–10).

It must have been wonderful to have heard this psalm sung in David's day.

COMPANIONS OF THE KING
WHO ENTER THE KINGDOM

Chorus of the Procession

> **The earth is the LORD'S, and the fulness thereof; the world, and they that dwell therein.**
> **For he hath founded it upon the seas, and established it upon the floods [Ps. 24:1–2].**

"The earth is the LORD'S." David speaks of Him again as the Creator. This earth belongs to Him. The earth does not belong to the Democrats or the Republicans. It does not belong to the president, whoever he might be. It does not belong to the Communists. There are so many people today who want to run this earth, but it belongs to God.

"He founded it upon the seas, and established it upon the floods." On the third day of creation God said, ". . . Let the waters under the heaven be gathered together unto one place, and let the dry land appear: and it was so. And God called the dry land Earth; and the gathering together of the waters called he Seas: and God saw that it was good" (Gen. 1:9–10). When God gathered the waters together, submerged land appeared out of the water. It was life out of death, and it speaks of resurrection.

Soloist

Who shall ascend into the hill of the LORD? or who shall stand in his holy place? [Ps. 24:3].

Who shall stand in his holy place? The answer is in the next verse.

Answering Soloist

He that hath clean hands, and a pure heart; who hath not lifted up his soul unto vanity, nor sworn deceitfully [Ps. 24:4].

If the only ones who are going to ascend into the hill of the Lord are those who have "clean hands and a pure heart," and those who have not "lifted up" their souls "unto vanity, nor sworn deceitfully," I guess I won't be there. That leaves me out. But I am going to be there, because I am going to be there in Christ. He has undertaken to present me before the throne of grace in His present priestly office because I have trusted Him as my Savior.

Chorus and Solo Voices

He shall receive the blessing from the LORD, and righteousness from the God of his salvation.

This is the generation of them that seek him, that seek thy face, O Jacob. Selah [Ps. 24:5–6].

Now picture this procession as it enters Jerusalem singing:

> **Lift up your heads, O ye gates; and be ye lift up, ye everlasting doors; and the King of glory shall come in [Ps. 24:7].**

A voice from the gates inquires: "Who is this King of glory?" And the chorus answers.

> **Who is this King of glory? The LORD strong and mighty, the LORD mighty in battle.**
>
> **Lift up your heads, O ye gates; even lift them up, ye everlasting doors; and the King of glory shall come in [Ps. 24:8-9].**

Another voice from the gates inquires: "Who is this King of glory?" And again the chorus answers—probably the full choir and orchestra.

> **Who is this King of glory? The LORD of hosts, he is the King of glory. Selah [Ps. 24:10].**

I think this passage illustrates two events. First of all this is a picture of when the Lord returned to heaven. It is also a picture of His coming to earth again. "Lift up your heads, O ye gates; even lift them up, ye everlasting doors; and the King of glory shall come in." Who is He? The world does not know, but this psalm gives us the answer. The King of glory is "The LORD strong and mighty, the LORD mighty in battle." Then the gates are told to open up so that the King of glory might enter in. Well, He is not "in" today. The world has rejected Him. "Who is this King of glory?" He is the Lord of hosts, He is the Lord Jesus Christ. He is King of kings and Lord of lords. And He is the King of glory. The psalmist writes "Selah" at the conclusion—that is, think on this for a little while. This will bless your heart, my beloved.

PSALM 25

THEME: Plea for mercy and deliverance

This psalm brings us to a new section. It begins a new series of
fifteen psalms—25 through 39—which primarily record David's
personal experience, but look also to the future when the godly remnant of Israel is in trouble. For the comfort of believers today they contain the balm of Gilead. The preceding psalms can be described as
dramatic and, in my judgment, sensational. But the following fifteen
psalms are more personal, quiet, and intimate. They have a wonderful
message and impact for our lives today. They are applicable to the
past, the present, and the future. Some of these psalms may not be so
familiar, but they have much to say to us. We will only be hitting the
high points, but there are many things to be learned. Often when I
could not sleep, or when I was away from home and in a strange place,
probably feeling a little lonely, I found myself turning to the Book of
Psalms, and particularly to this section, because it came out of the
experience of a man who was going through a time of trouble. It has a
prophetic element, and looks into the future to a time of trouble for the
faithful remnant of Israel, but it provides comfort to saints of all ages.

> **Unto thee, O LORD, do I lift up my soul.**
>
> **O my God, I trust in thee: let me not be ashamed, let not
> mine enemies triumph over me [Ps. 25:1–2].**

This is a prayer that reveals the dependence that David had upon God.
One day Israel will also experience this. The time will come when
that remnant of Israel will find themselves in a position where there is
no one upon whom they can depend but God. And it is good for us to
come to that place also.

When David says, "Unto thee, O LORD, do I lift up my soul," he is
getting right down to business. This is not just his voice talking, it is

his soul speaking. He continues, "O my God, I trust in thee: let me not be ashamed, let not mine enemies triumph over me." Have you ever been in a place where everything seemed to be failure rather than success? You did not want to go down in crushing defeat, either in your personal life, or your business life, or your home or church life. "Let not mine enemies triumph over me." What a prayer! Is this how you pray?

> **Yea, let none that wait on thee be ashamed: let them be ashamed which transgress without cause [Ps. 25:3].**

Now listen to his pleading.

> **Shew me thy ways, O LORD; teach me thy paths [Ps. 25:4].**

There are *two* ways a man can go. He can go God's way or his own way. God gives us a choice. We can walk in the path of our choosing. "There is a way which seemeth right unto a man, but the end thereof are the ways of death" (Prov. 14:12). What a glorious thing it is to be able to call out to God and ask Him to show us the way we should go.

> **Lead me in thy truth, and teach me: for thou art the God of my salvation; on thee do I wait all the day [Ps. 25:5].**

The psalmist is calling on God to show him the way, to teach him the way. This leads me to say that this is what is known as an acrostic psalm. That is, it is built upon the Hebrew alphabet. Each verse begins with a letter of the Hebrew alphabet. Unfortunately, in English we miss it.

> **Remember, O LORD, thy tender mercies and thy loving kindnesses; for they have been ever of old [Ps. 25:6].**

The psalmist speaks not only of the kindness of God but also of His loving kindnesses. It is difficult for me to distinguish between the two, but I think what a little girl once said in Sunday school is a good definition. She said, "When you ask your Mother for a piece of bread with butter on it, and she gives it to you, that is kindness. But when she puts jam on it without you asking her, that is loving kindness." I don't know of a better way to describe the difference. David could say this during a time of trouble, as will the godly remnant of Israel in their time of trouble. And this speaks to our hearts today. What was good for the saints of the past and will be good for the saints of the future is also good for us. I do not see how anyone could read the Psalms, or study the Epistle to the Romans, without seeing that God has a plan and purpose for the nation of Israel in the future. He is not yet through with His people.

> **Remember not the sins of my youth, nor my transgressions: according to thy mercy remember thou me for thy goodness' sake, O LORD [Ps. 25:7].**

David asked God not only to remember His tender mercies and loving kindnesses, but now he asks Him to forget something. He says, "Remember not the sins of my youth"—forget them. Then he prays to God for goodness and mercy. God is rich in both of these. He has enough for you today, and there will be some left over for me. I don't know about you, but I am going to need a whole lot of mercy; and I would like to have a lot of goodness, too. "Surely goodness and mercy shall follow me all the days of my life" (Ps. 23:6).

EXPRESSION OF CONFIDENCE IN GOD

In the second section of this psalm David expresses his confidence and trust.

> **Good and upright is the LORD: therefore will he teach sinners in the way.**
>
> **The meek will he guide in judgment: and the meek will he teach his way [Ps. 25:8–9].**

God's goodness, His love, and His righteousness are revealed in His provision for salvation for you and me.

For thy name's sake, O LORD, pardon mine iniquity; for it is great [Ps. 25:11].

God forgives us for Christ's sake, never for our sake. You and I do not merit forgiveness. We know that God forgave David; and, if we trust in the Lord Jesus Christ, He will forgive us, too. An old blasphemer came to me one time with a sneer on his face and asked "Why did God choose a man like David, who was such a big sinner?" I said to him, "You and I ought to take great comfort in that. If God would save David, there just might be a chance that He would save you and me." Concerning His people in the future, God says of Israel in Jeremiah 31:34, ". . . I will forgive their iniquity, and I will remember their sin no more."

The secret of the LORD is with them that fear him; and he will shew them his covenant [Ps. 25:14].

There are so many people today who are just question marks as far as their Christian lives are concerned. They don't understand this or that verse of Scripture, and they don't understand why God does certain things. Their lack of understanding is almost a dead giveaway. They are constantly in a questioning state. But "the secret of the LORD is with them that fear him." When we walk with the Lord, many times we do not need to ask a question; we just put our hand in His and walk along. My daughter and I often used to go for walks. She was a regular question-box. She had to ask questions about everything along the way. Finally she would grow tired, I would pick her up, and she would put her arms around my neck. Question time was over. She just accepted everything from then on. I think many of us should forget about some of the questions we have and simply put our hand in His and walk with Him.

TROUBLE AND DELIVERANCE

As we come to the final section of this psalm, we are faced once again with that time of trouble that is coming for Israel in the future.

> Mine eyes are ever toward the LORD; for he shall pluck my feet out of the net.
>
> Turn thee unto me, and have mercy upon me; for I am desolate and afflicted.
>
> The troubles of my heart are enlarged: O bring thou me out of my distresses [Ps. 25:15–17].

What a prayer this will be for the faithful remnant of Israel during the time of trouble that is coming. Also it is a good prayer for you and me when we experience times of trouble.

> Look upon mine affliction and my pain; and forgive all my sins [Ps. 25:18].

When we are in trouble we are more apt to confess our sins!

> Consider mine enemies; for they are many; and they hate me with cruel hatred.
>
> O keep my soul, and deliver me: let me not be ashamed; for I put my trust in thee.
>
> Let integrity and uprightness preserve me; for I wait on thee [Ps. 25:19–21].

Now hear the conclusion:

> Redeem Israel, O God, out of all his troubles [Ps. 25:22].

This glorious prayer is, you see, primarily for the nation Israel and for the day of trouble that is coming upon the earth.

All of us who are God's children have trouble during our lifetimes. This is a prayer for us. O God, deliver us out of all our troubles.

Years ago, down south, a black deacon got up and gave a testimony about a verse of Scripture that was meaningful to him. He said the verse was, "It came to pass." Everyone looked puzzled, so the preacher said to him, "How is it that that particular verse means so much to you?" "Well," the deacon said, "when I am in trouble, I always get my Bible and read, 'It came to pass,' and I thank God that my troubles came to *pass*, and they did not come to *stay*." That may not be the exact interpretation of those words, but it expresses the truth of Scripture, and that is exactly what Psalm 25 is saying. "Redeem Israel, O God, out of all his troubles." I am sure that you can see that the primary interpretation is for the nation Israel, but we certainly can also pray this prayer for ourselves.

PSALM 26

THEME: Plea on the basis of personal righteousness

In Psalm 25 David confessed his sins, and David was a great sinner. But in this psalm David talks about his righteousness. I don't know about you, but I have *perfect* righteousness—but it's not Vernon McGee's. First Corinthians 1:30 tells us, "But of him are ye in Christ Jesus, who of God is made unto us wisdom, and *righteousness,* and sanctification, and redemption." He has been made unto me righteousness as well as redemption. This is on the plus side of the ledger, and I stand complete in Him, accepted in the beloved. That is what it means to pray in His name. It is to present *His* work, *His* merit, and who *He* is with our requests.

> **Judge me, O Lord; for I have walked in mine integrity: I have trusted also in the Lord; therefore I shall not slide.**
>
> **Examine me, O Lord, and prove me; try my reins and my heart [Ps. 26:1–2].**

This is a marvelous psalm that speaks of David's walk. David committed a great sin, but David did not continue to live in sin. What David did once, the king of Babylon did every day. David's sin stands out like a lump of coal in a snowman because the rest of David's life was an example of godliness. He became a measuring stick for the kings who followed him. Every king was judged by whether or not he walked in the steps of his father David. If he followed David's example, he was accepted and proclaimed a good king.

This psalm reminds us of the first psalm. Notice how it reads: "Judge me, O Lord; for I have walked in mine integrity: I have trusted also in the Lord." It was because of his faith in the Lord that David did not slide. Not that he was so strong—he knew he wasn't—but he knew that when he trusted the Lord, the Lord would sustain him.

For thy lovingkindness is before mine eyes: and I have walked in thy truth.

I have not sat with vain persons, neither will I go in with dissemblers.

I have hated the congregation of evildoers; and will not sit with the wicked [Ps. 26:3–5].

This psalm is similar to Psalm 1 in content. David says, "I have walked in thy truth." This is a positive statement. Psalm 1 presents the negative side. "Blessed is the man that walketh *not* in the counsel of the ungodly" (v. 1). Furthermore, David states that he has "not sat with vain persons," nor "with dissemblers." David did not sit with false persons. As Psalm 1 put it, "Blessed is the man that walketh not in the counsel of the ungodly, nor standeth in the way of sinners, nor sitteth in the seat of the scornful" (v. 1).

I will wash mine hands in innocency: so will I compass thine altar, O Lord [Ps. 26:6].

A man's faith needs to be backed up by a good life. How important this psalm is in this connection—maybe the reason this section of psalms is not so popular today is because they emphasize a *life* that is pleasing to God.

My foot standeth in an even place: in the congregations will I bless the Lord [Ps. 26:12].

"My foot standeth in an even place." That means that he is sure-footed now. He is established on the Rock. The "even place" speaks of that. When you are on the side of a slippery hill, you are apt to fall. A lot of Christians are in that position today. They are playing with evil. They get close to it. It reminds me of a little boy in the pantry. His mother heard a noise in the back of the kitchen and asked, "Willie, where are you?" The boy replied, "I am in the pantry." She asked, "What are you doing?" He said, "I am fighting temptation." That was not the place for Willie to fight temptation!

Many Christians today flirt with sin. Some time ago I received a letter from one of our radio listeners who wanted counsel. She wrote about how her husband had died, and a close friend of her husband became the one to handle the estate. It was necessary for her to meet with him often; and before long—as she put it—the chemistry between them began to react, and they began to care for each other. She felt uneasy about the situation and asked what she should do. In my reply to her, I wrote: "You are in a burning building. Jump out as quickly as you can." I advised her to leave that town and relocate. Later I received another letter from her that said after a couple of weeks of rationalizing she had followed my suggestion and moved to another town. Looking back on it, she said, "I know I would have fallen if I had stayed there." My friend, it is well to have your feet on even ground. Where are you standing today? The reason a great many people fall is because they are fighting temptation in the pantry!

PSALM 27

THEME: Prayer

This is a deeply spiritual psalm and one that is very familiar to many of God's people. The moment you read the first verse your face will probably light up with recognition. It divides itself naturally into two major divisions. The first six verses speak of the provision God makes for the encouragement and confidence of His own. The remainder of the psalm is a prayer for help and sustenance. It is not a psalm for the super-duper saints but has a message for many hearts and lives. It is a prayer of David and opens on this grand note:

FOUNDATION FOR PRAYER

The Lord is my light and my salvation; whom shall I fear? the Lord is the strength of my life; of whom shall I be afraid? [Ps. 27:1].

This again is a "He and me" psalm. "The Lord is my light and my salvation."

"He is my light." He is a holy God. He is the One who directs and guides me by the light of His Word. Later the psalmist will say, "Thy word is a lamp unto my feet, and a light unto my path" (Ps. 119:105).

He is "my salvation," which speaks of the love of God, because it was His love that provided a salvation for us. That salvation, of course, is only through Jesus Christ. "For God so loved the world, that he gave his only begotten Son, that whosoever believeth in him should not perish, but have everlasting life" (John 3:16). God didn't so love the world that He saved the world; God so loved the world that He provided a salvation for sinners. And we have to come to Him on that basis. That salvation is conditioned, as Simon Peter put it: ". . . There is none other name under heaven given among men, whereby we must be saved" (Acts 4:12). This is the same salvation that David is talking about. "The LORD is my light and my salvation"—my *light*, my *salvation*.

"The LORD is the strength of my life." God not only gives life, He also empowers us to *live* that life on earth. Is He the light of your life, the One who loves you and gives you strength, my friend?

"Of whom shall I be afraid?" John Knox said, "One with God is a majority." When Cromwell was asked why he did not fear anyone, he said, "I have learned that if you fear God, you have no one else to fear."

> **When the wicked, even mine enemies and my foes, came upon me to eat up my flesh, they stumbled and fell [Ps. 27:2].**

David was probably looking back upon that time of his life when he was in much danger. He started out as a shepherd boy, and his life was in danger when he protected his sheep from a lion and a bear. That is something that a person does not do every day. I don't know about you, but I just don't meet a lion or a bear very often. When I do, they are on the other side of a cage. But there are people like lions and bears walking our streets today, many of them seeking to devour us. Also there is that old lion spoken of in 1 Peter 5:8, "Be sober, be vigilant; because your adversary the devil, as a roaring lion, walketh about, seeking whom he may devour."

> **Though an host should encamp against me, my heart shall not fear: though war should rise against me, in this will I be confident [Ps. 27:3].**

David's confidence was in God, and this is the provision that God has made for His own today. Have you ever noticed that every time the Lord Jesus would break through to speak to His apostles after His resurrection He would say, "Fear not"? You and I have a resurrected Savior. Fear comes to us many times. I have a natural fear of heights; and when I am flying in that big bus in the sky, I say to the Lord, "You are with me. My confidence is in You."

MEDITATION ON PRAYER

One thing have I desired of the Lord, that will I seek after; that I may dwell in the house of the Lord all the days of my life, to behold the beauty of the Lord, and to inquire in his temple [Ps. 27:4].

This is a rich verse. David had whittled his life down to one point: "One thing have I desired of the Lord." Also Paul did that with his life. He said, ". . . but this one thing I do, forgetting those things which are behind, and reaching forth unto those things which are before, I press toward the mark for the prize of the high calling of God in Christ Jesus" (Phil. 3:13–14). In this day, whittle down your life, as you would whittle down a pencil, until you can write with it. Our lives are very complicated, so just keep whittling. Most of my life I felt like Martha in the kitchen. She was encumbered with much service (see Luke 10:40). Poor Martha reached for a pot to cook something in it; then she reached for a pan to boil something in it, and she reached for another container to put the potatoes in, and by that time something fell out of the cupboard. She became frustrated trying to do everything at once. How complicated life has become for many of us. We are frustrated, under tension and pressure all the time. It is wonderful to whittle your life down to what is important. It is a relief to reduce your life to the lowest common denominator. I hope you won't mind my speaking out of personal experience, but the happiest time of my ministry began when I retired from the pastorate; the most spiritually profitable time of my life began at that moment. I have seen more folk turn to Christ in this brief interval than in any other period of my life, and I have never rejoiced so. Do you know why? I have whittled my life down to the one thing I want to do—teach the Bible. That is all I am doing. My life has been whittled down to that, and I am enthusiastic about it. I believe this is what God wants me to do.

Now notice the "one thing" in David's life was "that I may dwell in the house of the Lord all the days of my life." Now I don't think David intended to take his sleeping bag into the tabernacle and stay there. But he wanted the ark, which was God's meeting place with His people, with him in Jerusalem. He went to great lengths to bring it to Jerusalem and erected a tabernacle for it and planned an elaborate temple for God. Why? Through that he had *access* to God. That was the "one thing" in David's life.

We have access to God through Christ, and this is the thing we ought to rejoice in. He is the One who will enable us to whittle our lives down to that one point. Paul gives us the eight benefits of being justified by faith in Romans 5:1-5. The second benefit Paul mentions is access to God: "By whom also we have access by faith into this grace wherein we stand, and rejoice in hope of the glory of God." What a wonderful thing it is to have access to God!

This is the one thing that was the aim of David's life. "One thing have I desired of the LORD, that will I seek after; that I may dwell in the house of the LORD all the days of my life, to behold the beauty of the LORD, and to inquire in his temple." In the house of God was the mercy seat. David needed mercy, and I need mercy—and I am sure you do also. In the house of God was an altar that spoke of the cross of Christ. This provided for David *access* into the presence of God. You and I can approach God through the Lord Jesus today. We have access into this marvelous grace. What a privilege is ours to have access to God!

No wonder this psalm has been such a wonderful blessing to God's people. Now notice this fifth verse:

For in the time of trouble he shall hide me in his pavilion: in the secret of his tabernacle shall he hide me; he shall set me up upon a rock [Ps. 27:5].

Where was the secret place of the tabernacle? It was inside the Holy of Holies. No one could go there but the high priest. Do you know what was in there? The ark of the covenant, which was only a box overlaid with gold; but upon the ark was the elaborate lid, which God designated as the mercy seat because blood was sprinkled upon it. Now in our day because the Lord Jesus has shed His blood, we have a mercy seat to which we can go. And that is where He hides us. What a secure place we have!

> **And now shall mine head be lifted up above mine enemies round about me: therefore will I offer in his tabernacle sacrifices of joy; I will sing, yea, I will sing praises unto the LORD [Ps. 27:6].**

When we get this wonderful picture and recognize what He has done for us, it will put a song in our hearts. This leads him to pray the next verse.

DECLARATION OF PRAYER PROPER

> **Hear, O LORD, when I cry with my voice: have mercy also upon me, and answer me [Ps. 27:7].**

You see, in that secret place there was mercy. And God has prepared that secret place for us today where we can receive the mercy of God.

> **When thou saidst, Seek ye my face; my heart said unto thee, Thy face, LORD, will I seek [Ps. 27:8].**

David puts the invitation in the Lord's mouth. When God said, "Seek ye my face," David said, "I have already responded. My heart said unto Thee, 'Thy face, LORD, will I seek.'" My friend, God has a longing for you. Do you respond to that? It is awful to live with a person who does not express his love. Marriage is not an arrangement whereby a woman gets a living and a man gets a cook. Marriage is a love relationship; if it is not that, it isn't anything. Our relationship to God should be like that. David's heart responded when God said, "I love you." David said, "I love You." When God said, "I want to have fellowship with you," David said, "I want to have fellowship with You."

> **Hide not thy face far from me; put not thy servant away in anger: thou hast been my help; leave me not, neither forsake me, O God of my salvation [Ps. 27:9].**

When David sinned, he found out what it was like for God to hide His face from him. He lost his fellowship. He lost his joy. But he prayed, "Restore unto me the *joy* of my salvation."
The next verse has been misunderstood.

When my father and my mother forsake me, then the LORD will take me up [Ps. 27:10].

This verse has been misunderstood by critics. Even Delitzsch suggested that this verse could have been written by someone else. The reason that possibility is considered is because David's father and mother did not forsake him. But I do not think that is what David is saying here. You will notice that this is a temporal clause—"When my father and my mother." It would be better translated "*Had* my father and my mother forsaken me, then the Lord will take me up." I wish the new revisions of the Bible would call attention to that fact. Probably your father and mother have not forsaken you—but should they do so, then the Lord would take you up.

Some wiseacre said, "When my father and my mother forsake me, then the *boy scouts* will take me up." I am afraid that many parents are letting organizations, including the church, raise their children. Even though you may be a member of a good Bible church, your children are *yours.* You are the one who should lead them to the Lord, not the Sunday school teacher or the preacher—*you.* And *you* are the one who should give them your time and attention.

Teach me thy way, O LORD, and lead me in a plain path, because of mine enemies [Ps. 27:11].

David is saying, "I want a good testimony before the enemy, because I know he will criticize me. I want You to watch over me, Lord, and help me not to embarrass You by what I do."

Deliver me not over unto the will of mine enemies: for false witnesses are risen up against me, and such as breathe out cruelty [Ps. 27:12].

I was brought up in a denomination that has since gone into liberalism. And I was a preacher in a denomination that has gone into liberalism. I always prayed to the Lord, "Do not let me fall into a position where I am at the mercy of church leaders or a church board." I was an active pastor from about 1930 to 1970. During that entire time of forty years, God never let me get into a position where I was at the mercy of men. That is what David is praying in this verse. My heart goes out to many ministers today who find themselves at the mercy of a church board or some hierarchy. I urge them to pray like David did, "Don't deliver me into the will of my enemies. Don't let them get me down and pin my shoulders to the mat, Lord." I think He will hear and answer that prayer.

REALIZATION OF PRAYER

I had fainted, unless I had believed to see the goodness of the LORD in the land of the living [Ps. 27:13].

Even in the world today you can see the goodness of the Lord. How wonderful He is.

Wait on the LORD: be of good courage, and he shall strengthen thine heart: wait, I say, on the LORD [Ps. 27:14].

There is a lot of heart trouble today among believers. It is known as faintheartedness, or the coward's heart. All of us have a little touch of it. How can this be cured? "Wait on the LORD; be of good courage." When we do that the Lord will strengthen our hearts. He is really the great heart specialist.

PSALM 28

THEME: A cry in the time of trouble

This wonderful little psalm contains a cry—David is in trouble here. And it is prophetic of Israel during the Tribulation. It is a prayer for judgment upon his enemies and praise for the deliverance he knows will come. This psalm is actually preliminary to the next one.

> Unto thee will I cry, O LORD my rock; be not silent to me: lest, if thou be silent to me, I become like them that go down into the pit [Ps. 28:1].

Israel knew about the "Rock." This Rock Israel rejected, as Moses lamented, ". . . then he [Israel] forsook God which made him, and lightly esteemed the Rock of his salvation" (Deut. 32:15). A rock is something to stand upon. It provides a sure foundation. The believer in our day also knows about that Rock. The apostle Paul wrote, "For other foundation can no man lay than that is laid, which is Jesus Christ" (1 Cor. 3:11).

> Hear the voice of my supplications, when I cry unto thee, when I lift up my hands toward thy holy oracle [Ps. 28:2].

The "holy oracle" was the mercy seat, which was in the tabernacle. The mercy seat Christ has provided is what you and I need to cling to today.

> Blessed be the LORD, because he hath heard the voice of my supplications [Ps. 28:6].

God hears and answers prayer. As a result, David now says:

> **The LORD is my strength and my shield; my heart trusted in him, and I am helped: therefore my heart greatly rejoiceth; and with my song will I praise him.**
>
> **The LORD is their strength, and he is the saving strength of his anointed.**
>
> **Save thy people, and bless thine inheritance: feed them also, and lift them up for ever [Ps. 28:7-9].**

God is power; He is mighty. And He is a shield for protection. He is power and protection. But you say, "Is He my power? Is He my protection?" He is if your heart trusts in Him. If you trust God, He will help you. He will hear and answer prayer.

What happens when He answers prayer? "With my song will I praise him." Oh, my friend, let's not forget to thank Him and praise Him when He answers our prayers!

He is "the saving strength of his anointed"—the "anointed" is the Messiah, Christ, who is so often mentioned in the Psalms as the coming Deliverer for Israel.

He concludes with this plea, "Save thy people," or another translation is "Shepherd thy people." The anointed One is their Shepherd who will "lift them up forever" when He comes. It reminds us of what Isaiah wrote, "He shall feed his flock like a shepherd: he shall gather the lambs with his arm, and carry them in his bosom, and shall gently lead those that are with young" (Isa. 40:11).

PSALM 29

THEME: *The voice of the Lord in a thunderstorm*

The psalm before us is a nature psalm. It is not the first nature psalm, as we have already read Psalm 8: "When I consider thy heavens, the work of thy fingers, the moon and the stars, which thou hast ordained," which is a psalm to be read on a good clear night. Then we read Psalm 19, "The heavens declare the glory of God; and the firmament sheweth his handiwork." Then he likens the sun to a bridegroom coming out of his chamber. That is a daytime psalm. Now we come to a psalm that describes a storm. In this psalm is the gloom of the tempest, the clap of thunder, the flash of lightning, and terror on every side. Several years ago a hurricane which they named Camille hit the Gulf Coast. She hurled her might on the other side of New Orleans, around Gulfport, Mississippi. Camille caused millions of dollars worth of damage. In an apartment in that area, several couples decided to have a hurricane party. It was a great beer bust, and I suppose they all got drunk. I understand that most of them were killed when the storm hit. It is too bad to go into eternity like that. I wish they had read Psalm 29 instead. My friend, if you are frightened in a storm, rather than trying to get your courage from a bottle, I suggest you read this magnificent psalm. It has a message in the time of storm.

The structure of this psalm is quite interesting. This is Hebrew poetry of the highest order. Ewald said of this psalm, "This psalm is elaborated with a symmetry of which no more perfect specimen exists in Hebrew." Delitzsch called it "The Psalm of seven thunders." Perowne said this about it: "This Psalm is a magnificent description of a thunderstorm. Its mighty march from north to south, the desolation and terror which it causes, the peal of thunder, the flash of lightning, even the gathering fury and lull of the elements, are vividly depicted."

So Psalm 29 is a song of Hebrew poetry describing a storm. Hebrew poetry is not attained by rhyming. When we think of poetry, we think of rhymes. We like the sentences to end in words that sound alike. Here is an example of one of our modern ditties: "I shoot the hippopotamus with bullets made of platinum. If I used lead ones, his hide were sure to flatten 'em!" That is not exactly Shakespeare, but it is our kind of poetry. Hebrew poetry is attained by what is known as parallelism, which is repeating a thought in a different way and generally amplifying and enlarging upon it.

The psalm sweeps along with all the freedom and majesty of a storm. There is sort of a lilting triumph here, a glorious abandon, a courageous exultation.

The first two verses are the prologue: "Give unto the LORD, O ye mighty, give unto the LORD glory and strength. Give unto the LORD the glory due unto his name; worship the LORD in the beauty of holiness." David lifts our thoughts to the very highest.

Now, the epilogue is the last two verses: "The LORD sitteth upon the flood; yea, the LORD sitteth King for ever. The LORD will give strength unto his people; the LORD will bless his people with peace." The storm with all its fury lashed across the land, but Jehovah was still in control. And, my friend, in the storms of life He is still in control.

Before we look at this psalm in detail, let me say a word about the subject (which is developed in vv. 3–10). Seven times the voice of the Lord is mentioned: "The voice of the LORD is upon the waters . . . the voice of the LORD is powerful . . . the voice of the LORD is full of majesty . . . the voice of the LORD breaketh the cedars" and so on.

Notice the setting of this psalm. David wrote it. He was an outdoorsman. He was not bottled up in an office. He was not held down to a throne. However, when this storm came, he was not outside; he was in Jerusalem, a city that was beautifully situated. David was in his cedar palace built on Mount Zion, the highest point. He could view the whole land. He could look to the northeast and see the clouds beginning to gather and watch as the storm was getting ready to break. I think most of us are acquainted with the geography of the Holy Land. If you are not, turn to the map in the back of your Bible that shows the location of Jerusalem.

As you look at your map, you will see that the Mediterranean Sea is on your left to the west. Up north there are two ranges of mountains: the Lebanon and the Anti-Lebanon. There is Mount Carmel up there at Haifa and Mount Hermon, the Sea of Galilee on the east, the Valley of Esdraelon, the Jordan River and the Dead Sea. Then there is Mount Ebal and Mount Gerizim in Samaria and the rugged terrain lying immediately north. Bethel, Ai, and Anathoth are just north of Jerusalem. In Jerusalem you look to the west and see Joppa, to the east you see Jericho, and to the south you see the wilderness of Judea, frightful and ominous. David and Amos knew how to survive in that wilderness—a bishop from San Francisco several years ago didn't know; and he perished there. From David's palace on Mount Zion, the highest point in the city of Jerusalem, he could look over this landscape.

PROLOGUE

Give unto the LORD, O ye mighty, give unto the LORD glory and strength.

Give unto the LORD the glory due unto his name; worship the LORD in the beauty of holiness [Ps. 29:1–2].

Notice that the psalm is addressed to the "mighty." I agree with Bishop Horne that "the prophet addresses himself to the 'mighty ones of the earth,' exhorting them to 'give' God the glory and to submit themselves to the kingdom of the Messiah."

SUBJECT

Now we come to the substance of the psalm. The thunderstorm sweeps over the entire land.

We have three strophes, or stanzas, here.

The voice of the LORD is upon the waters: the God of glory thundereth: the LORD is upon many waters.

The voice of the LORD is powerful; the voice of the LORD is full of majesty [Ps. 29:3–4].

That is the beginning of the storm. Way up in the northwest there is distant thunder and lightning. The storm is gathering. The storm begins to move down toward Jerusalem and the voice of Jehovah is the thunder. In the palace David sees the gathering storm. He hears the wind begin to blow. The clouds become black and angry. They hide the sun and it is dark at midday. There is the low rumble of thunder and the flash of lightning which is streaked and forked. This is not a summer shower. This is not an ordinary storm. It is like the hurricane Camille I mentioned earlier. The storm breaks on the Mediterranean Coast. The waves roll high and break with the sound of a cannon on the shore. The angry waves mount up, and then the storm strikes inland. You can see its mighty march from north to south. Jerusalem will not escape it—it comes closer and closer. "The voice of the Lord is powerful." You can now hear that thunder. It shakes everything. "The voice of the Lord is full of majesty"—it is awe-inspiring.

The voice of the LORD breaketh the cedars; yea, the LORD breaketh the cedars of Lebanon [Ps. 29:5].

As the thunder rolls and rumbles, Lebanon is shaken. The trees are struck by lightning. Mighty Mount Hermon is shaken like a dog shakes a rabbit. As the storm draws nearer to Jerusalem, its approach is majestic and awe-inspiring. It rolls along with the rhythm of the thunder and lightning over the hills. Here it comes, as it begins to roll.

He maketh them also to skip like a calf; Lebanon and Sirion like a young unicorn.

The voice of the LORD divideth the flames of fire [Ps. 29:6–7].

The lightning is near Jerusalem now. It pops and crackles like heavy guns in a battle. The storm breaks with all its fury. In Jerusalem the streets are deserted. Shutters are slammed. A hush settles over the city. It is the hush before the sledgehammer blow comes. Only the barking of a dog in the Kidron Valley can be heard. Suddenly it comes.

Rain descends in torrents. Savage winds hurl themselves against the walls of Jerusalem. A shutter breaks loose. It bangs and makes a tremendous noise. David has been through this before. He waits patiently and listens to the voice of Jehovah.

The voice of the LORD shaketh the wilderness; the LORD shaketh the wilderness of Kadesh [Ps. 29:8].

Now David sees the storm passing over. It moves away, and the rains let up, and the winds die down. The storm is departing, and the people begin to open their shutters. The storm is departing from Jerusalem and advancing upon the wilderness of Judea to the south and west. Kadesh is down there. Soon the storm is spent in the wilderness of Sinai. The air is fresh, and David can hear the roar of water down in the Kidron Valley.

The voice of the LORD maketh the hinds to calve, and discovereth the forests: and in his temple doth every one speak of his glory [Ps. 29:9].

The storm did accomplish some good. Animals were frightened, causing some that were carrying young to give birth—there was no prolonged pain. It also caused some people to go to the temple who had not been there for a long time. They went to the temple to call upon God. The storm has died away and has disappeared in the south.

EPILOGUE

The LORD sitteth upon the flood; yea, the LORD sitteth King for ever [Ps. 29:10].

God was in charge of this storm all of the time, just as He was in charge of the flood.

The LORD will give strength unto his people; the LORD will bless his people with peace [Ps. 29:11].

The power of God in a storm is great, and it is He who gives strength during a storm. God can strengthen and enable us to go through the storms of life and know what peace is afterward. The storm with all of its fury may lash across the land, but Jehovah is still in control. In every storm of life He is in control, and He will bless His people with peace.

As we have gone through the Psalms, I have called attention to the fact that the Great Tribulation lies ahead for Israel, but God will see His people through it. Armageddon is ahead for these people. The enemy will come from the north and will cover the land, but God is in the storm, and He is in control. What a message this is for Israel.

This psalm has a message for us. We belong to a new creation. We do not belong to the old creation. We belong to the last Adam. "Therefore if any man be in Christ, he is a new creature [creation]: old things are passed away; behold, all things are become new" (2 Cor. 5:17). That is the reason I do not keep the Sabbath day—it belongs to the old creation. You hear the question: "When was the Sabbath day changed?" It was never changed. We have been changed and are now joined to a living Christ. Our new day to worship is the first day of the week, the day of resurrection. Adam was given dominion over creation, but he lost it. Christ has recovered it, and the old creation furnishes us with a pattern, an illustration, and the message is here for us today.

There are storms in the new creation, spiritual storms, storms that threaten to destroy us. If you are God's child, you have been through storms, or you are in a storm even now. The last Adam, Jesus Christ, is master of storms. He went through storms with His own. Once when He and His disciples were in a boat, a storm came up on the Sea of Galilee. "And there arose a great storm of wind, and the waves beat into the ship, so that it was now full. And he was in the hinder part of the ship, asleep on a pillow: and they awake him, and say unto him, Master, carest thou not that we perish? And he arose, and rebuked the wind, and said unto the sea, Peace, be still. And the wind ceased, and there was a great calm. And he said unto them, Why are ye so fearful? how is it that ye have no faith?" (Mark 4:37–40). In this instance the Lord quieted the storm, but He does not always do that. Sometimes He just whispers to us, "We are going to make it to the harbor." That is important.

I can think of many people who are in the storm today. There is a little Eskimo mother way up yonder in Alaska. She listens to our Thru the Bible Radio program. She lost a son in Vietnam. She is snowed in in the winter, and she wrote to tell me that listening to the Word being taught is helping to carry her through this difficult time. She is in a storm, but God will see her through it. One of these days the storm is going to be over.

I know of a family in Southern California which is going through a storm. A broker in San Francisco wrote and told me that he would have lost his mind if it was not for the fact that the Lord Jesus stood by him. I was in Flagstaff, Arizona, some time ago and, while I was there, a storm gathered. By the time I was ready to leave on the train (I thank the Lord I was not flying), oh! the thunder, lightning, and the rain were furious. But before I arrived at my destination, the storm passed, and the moon came out. It was so wonderful, so beautiful. Are you going through a storm? There are two things you should remember: the storm will end, and the Lord will see you through it.

PSALM 30

THEME: Hallelujah for healing

This is a psalm and song at the dedication of the house of David. It is a song of praise and worship. After the storm of life is over, there is a song. Some Bible scholars have thought that David wrote this when he brought up the ark to Jerusalem and placed it in the tabernacle he had erected for it. Others have thought that it was written for the dedication of the threshing floor of Araunah, the area where the future temple was to be built. Still others believe it has a prophetic aspect and was David's expression of praise and thanksgiving when God promised to build him a house (2 Sam. 7:11). It is interesting to note that in the modern Jewish ritual it is used at the Feast of *Chanukah,* the Feast of Dedication, which dates back to the time of the Maccabees.

> **I will extol thee, O LORD; for thou hast lifted me up, and hast not made my foes to rejoice over me.**
>
> **O LORD my God, I cried unto thee, and thou hast healed me [Ps. 30:1–2].**

It is my belief, and the belief of many others, that David was once as sick as Hezekiah, and God raised him up. We have no record of what his sickness might have been, but these verses tell us that God healed him. I like this psalm because God did the same thing for me. In fact, I consider this my psalm, because after having cancer, the Lord has permitted me to live. "O LORD my God, I cried unto thee, and thou hast healed me." Perhaps I should organize a chorus and call it "The Cancer Chorus," of those folk all across the country who have been attacked by the awful monster of cancer and God has sustained them.

> O LORD, thou hast brought up my soul from the grave:
> thou hast kept me alive, that I should not go down to the
> pit [Ps. 30:3].

I don't know about you, but I could sing, or at least say, this psalm. It has a great deal of meaning to me.

> Sing unto the LORD, O ye saints of his, and give thanks at
> the remembrance of his holiness [Ps. 30:4].

We "give thanks at the remembrance of his holiness." God didn't heal me because I am some special little pet of His. He didn't heal me because I am a teacher of the Bible. He did it because He is a holy God and He maintains His holiness. He recognizes my sins, and He has saved me by His grace. He hasn't lowered His standard one bit. Again I say, Hallelujah for healing; I praise Him, my Great Physician. I don't have to praise some great man or woman who claims to be a healer. I didn't go to a person like that. I went directly to the Great Physician. Oh, my friend, if you are sick, take your case to the Great Physician, and then call in the best doctor you can get—because our Great Physician gave him all the skill and wisdom he has (whether or not he recognizes that fact). God is holy. We ought to be thankful that we have a holy God who deals with us in grace.

> For his anger endureth but a moment; in his favour is
> life: weeping may endure for a night, but joy cometh in
> the morning [Ps. 30:5].

"His anger endureth but a moment." The storm will be over. Even if God judges me, His anger endures only for a moment. The Lord has taken me to the woodshed on two or three occasions. My dad used to take me to the woodshed, and I was accustomed to it. He died when I was fourteen years old. Shortly after that, I came to know the Lord as my Savior; and He has been taking me to the woodshed ever since. It is not pleasant to be punished, but His anger does not last forever; it only lasts for a moment.

> I cried to thee, O LORD; and unto the LORD I made suppli-
> cation.
>
> What profit is there in my blood, when I go down to the
> pit? Shall the dust praise thee? shall it declare thy truth?
> [Ps. 30:8–9].

I told the Lord the same thing David did. I said, "Lord, I would love to stay in this life and teach Your Word. I am going to be with You a long time when I get to heaven, but I would love to stay on earth a little while longer." David talked like that, and I feel akin to him.

Friend, you will find a psalm that fits you. I believe that every person can find a psalm that will be just his size. This one is my size.

> To the end that my glory may sing praise to thee, and not
> be silent. O LORD my God, I will give thanks unto thee
> for ever [Ps. 30:12].

There is nothing I could say to improve this verse. What David said, I want to say. I hope it is what you want to say, too. David's life had changed. He went from sickness to health, from mourning to gladness, and from silence to praise.

PSALM 31

THEME: A prayer of deliverance from trouble

Most of the psalms are very unfamiliar; yet they comprise one of the richest portions of God's Word. My feeling is that if proper emphasis were given in this section, it would give a different perspective to Scripture, especially relative to God's purposes in the nation Israel.

Practically all of the psalms we have looked at so far have been written by David, and he probably composed the music that went with them. Each psalm has a special meaning for each of us. Here again we see the troubles of the godly. So far in the Psalms there has been a lot of that; but, after all, the godly do have a lot of troubles—at least the ones I know have troubles. Psalm 31 speaks particularly of the past troubles of David. Also it looks to the future and refers prophetically to the troubles that will come to the nation Israel in the Great Tribula- tion. Finally, it speaks of the present troubles that we have. Th.. , psalm has a message for you and for me. At night when I cannot sleep. I generally turn to the Psalms, particularly to this section. Here I find great comfort and help.

> **In thee, O Lord, do I put my trust; let me never be ashamed: deliver me in thy righteousness [Ps. 31:1].**

"Deliver me in thy *righteousness*." David knew that God could not lower His standards in order to save sinners. Sin required a penalty; and, if the sinner did not pay it, someone else would have to pay it. God has a plan, and He can save sinners because Someone else has paid the penalty for sin. That Person is His Son, Jesus Christ. Because of this, David goes on to say:

> **Bow down thine ear to me; deliver me speedily: be thou my strong rock, for an house of defence to save me [Ps. 31:2].**

We need a strong rock—not just some little pebble. "He saith unto them, But whom say ye that I am? And Simon Peter answered and said, Thou art the Christ, the Son of the living God. And Jesus answered and said unto him, Blessed art thou, Simon Bar-jona: for flesh and blood hath not revealed it unto thee, but my Father which is in heaven. And I say also unto thee, That thou art Peter, and upon this rock I will build my church; and the gates of hell shall not prevail against it" (Matt. 16:15–18). The Rock upon which the church is built is Christ. "For other foundation can no man lay than that is laid, which is Jesus Christ" (1 Cor. 3:11). The Savior, Jesus Christ, is the strong Rock upon which we can rest. I am reminded of the little Scottish lady who was talking about her salvation and her assurance of it: "There are times when I am frightened and I tremble on the Rock, but the Rock never trembles under me." It is a strong Rock.

Now David is not yet through with the Rock. He has more to say. Maybe you could call this the first "rock" music, although it is a little different from the kind we hear today.

For thou art my rock and my fortress; therefore for thy name's sake lead me, and guide me [Ps. 31:3].

Is the Lord God your Rock? Is that where you are resting today? Is He your fortress? A fortress is for protection. You need that.

"Therefore for thy *name's sake* lead me, and guide me"—not because I am David the king, but for *His name's* sake.

Pull me out of the net that they have laid privily for me: for thou art my strength [Ps. 31:4].

"Pull me out of the net that they have laid privily [secretly] for me."

Into thine hand I commit my spirit: thou hast redeemed me, O LORD God of truth [Ps. 31:5].

At the scene of our Lord's crucifixion we are told, "And when Jesus had cried with a loud voice, he said, Father, into thy hands I commend

my spirit: and having said thus, he gave up the ghost" (Luke 23:46).
When Stephen, the first martyr, was stoned to death, we are told in
Acts 7:59, "And they stoned Stephen, calling upon God, and saying,
Lord Jesus, receive my spirit." It is interesting that down through the
history of the church many martyrs have used that same expression.
For instance, when the sentence of degradation was being executed
upon John Huss, the bishop pronounced upon him these horrible
words: "And now we commit thy soul to the devil." And John Huss, in
great calmness, stood there and replied, "I commit my spirit into Thy
hands, Lord Jesus Christ. Unto Thee I commend my spirit whom Thou
hast redeemed." When Polycarp was being burned at the stake in
Smyrna, these were also his words. Bernard used them; Jerome of
Prague used them; Luther and Melancthon and many others have also
used them. In fact, Martin Luther said, "Blessed are they who die not
only for the Lord, as martyrs; not only in the Lord as believers, but
likewise *with* the Lord, as breathing forth their lives in the words, into
Thy hands I commend my spirit."

> **I will be glad and rejoice in thy mercy: for thou hast
> considered my trouble; thou hast known my soul in ad-
> versities [Ps. 31:7].**

Dr. Gaebelein changed this verse a little: "Thou hast *seen* my troubles;
Thou hast *seen* my soul in adversities." I like that better. Twice the
psalmist says it. There is great comfort in knowing that God sees you
in your trouble. Remember that God said to Moses when He wanted to
deliver the children of Israel out of Egypt: ". . . I have surely *seen* the
affliction of my people which are in Egypt, and have heard their cry
by reason of their taskmasters; for I know their sorrows; And I am
come down to deliver them out of the hand of the Egyptians . . ."
(Exod. 3:7–8). The Lord had seen the affliction of His people. He had
heard their groaning. He knew their condition, and He came down to
deliver them.

The Gospels record the time the disciples were out on the Sea of
Galilee in a boat when they were hit by a storm. It was the dead of
night, and the waves were rolling high. They thought it was the end

for them. But Mark says, concerning the Lord, "And he *saw* them toiling in rowing; for the wind was contrary unto them . . ." (Mark 6:48). I like that. He sees you and me today. He knows our troubles. What a comfort this is.

Now we come to a prayer.

> **Have mercy upon me, O Lord, for I am in trouble: mine eye is consumed with grief, yea, my soul and my belly [Ps. 31:9].**

Are you in trouble, friend? Instead of whining and telling everybody else about it, why don't you go to the Lord? Say, "Lord, I am in trouble!" That is what David did.

> **My times are in thy hand: deliver me from the hand of mine enemies, and from them that persecute me [Ps. 31:15].**

"My times are in thy hand" is an interesting expression. Many people go to fortune-tellers and have their palms read. They are told that this line means this and another line means something else. All of it is perfect nonsense, but it affords a living for some people; and for others who are trying to get rid of money it provides another way of getting rid of it. But our times are in Christ's hands. "My times are in thy hand"—and those are crucified hands. I can see my sin in His hands. And they are the tender hands of a Shepherd. He picked up a lost sheep and put it on His shoulders. My care and protection are in those hands. Some future day He is coming with blessing, and those hands will bless. I rejoice that my times are in His hands.

> **Make thy face to shine upon thy servant: save me for thy mercies' sake [Ps. 31:16].**

"Make thy face to shine upon thy servant" is a lovely expression. A Hebrew commentator back in ancient times said, "The face of God is his Anointed, the Messiah." You see, God is a spirit. I don't know how

He looks or how He feels or how He acts. But the Lord Jesus came down here to show us the Father. He is the face of God. Through Him we know God. It reminds me of the little girl whose mother took her upstairs and tucked her in bed for the night. Soon after she left her, the child began to whimper, and she called to her, "You go to sleep. God is up there with you." But the little girl wanted someone to stay with her. Once again her mother told her, "God is up there with you." To this the little girl replied, "I know, but I want somebody with a *face!*" My friend, that is what all of us need. All of us little children down here want Somebody with a face to be with us. Jesus Christ is God with a face. How wonderful!

> **Oh how great is thy goodness, which thou hast laid up for them that fear thee; which thou hast wrought for them that trust in thee before the sons of men! [Ps. 31:19].**

How great is the goodness of the Lord! Have you ever told anyone how good God is? Psalm 107:1–2 says, "O give thanks unto the LORD, for he is good: for his mercy endureth for ever. Let the redeemed of the LORD say so, whom he hath redeemed from the hand of the enemy." I find that people like to talk about their neighbors or their children or their father and mother or relatives or their boss or their preacher, but not many people like to talk about the goodness of God. My, how good He is! When was the last time you told someone how good God is?

PSALM 32

THEME: *A psalm of instruction*

This psalm has been called a spiritual gem; yet it has been misunderstood. The title is: "A Psalm of David, Maschil." *Maschil* means "to give instruction" or "to understand." This Hebrew word is used especially as it relates to the future of Israel. I can't help but think of the seminaries today that have gone intellectual, depending on high-powered personalities and promotional programs and that type of thing to sell themselves. They emphasize the intellectual. It would be nice if they would turn to this psalm and find out that God has a future for Israel, but it requires a little spiritual gumption to get the point.

I want you to see how the word *maschil* is used in connection with the nation Israel. In Daniel 11:33 we read, "And they that understand [*maschil*] among the people shall instruct many: yet they shall fall by the sword, and by flame, by captivity, and by spoil, many days." Again, in Daniel 11:35 we read, "And some of them of understanding [*maschil*] shall fall, to try them, and to purge, and to make them white, even to the time of the end: because it is yet for a time appointed." Daniel 12:3 says, "And they that be wise [*maschil*] shall shine as the brightness of the firmament; and they that turn many to righteousness as the stars for ever and ever." In Daniel 12:10 we read, "Many shall be purified, and made white, and tried; but the wicked shall do wickedly: and none of the wicked shall understand; but the wise [*maschil*] shall understand."

In the New Testament, the Lord Jesus, in speaking of the time of the trouble coming in the future for the nation Israel, says in Matthew 24:15, "When ye therefore shall see the abomination of desolation, spoken of by Daniel the prophet, stand in the holy place, (whoso readeth, let him understand [*maschil*]:)." The Lord was saying that when they see the abomination of desolation spoken of by Daniel the prophet, it is time to run for their lives. I don't know what the abomination of desolation is. I have read quite a few books by men who thought they knew what it is. It took some of them two or three chapters to make it clear that they didn't know what it is. I can say it in one sentence: I don't know what it is. I am not looking for the abomination of desolation; I am looking for the Lord Jesus Christ. Notice that at the end of Matthew 24:15 the Lord said, ". . . whoso readeth, let him understand."

In the Book of Revelation, chapters 6–18, we are told more about the Great Tribulation period. In Revelation 13, which tells us about two beasts and the world dictatorship that is coming, we read, "Here is wisdom. Let him that hath understanding count the number of the beast: for it is the number of a man; and his number is Six hundred threescore and six" (Rev. 13:18). Numerous books have been written about the number 666. Do you want to know what that number means? I can give you an answer: I don't know! Those who have written the books about the number 666 don't know either—they just think they know. It will be a day when God will reveal Himself to His people. Psalm 32 is a maschil psalm. It will be instruction for God's people in a future day. Right now it is a psalm of instruction for us.

Psalm 32 has been called a penitential psalm, that is, a confession of David. I disagree with that. Psalm 51 is David's prayer of confession after Nathan said to him, 'Thou art the man" (2 Sam. 12:7). In that psalm he asks for forgiveness. In Psalm 32 is the record of the confession, the forgiveness received, and the blessedness of his complete restoration. In Psalm 51:12–13 David says, "Restore unto me the joy of thy salvation; and uphold me with thy free spirit. Then will I teach transgressors thy ways; and sinners shall be converted unto thee." David promises if the Lord will forgive him for his sin that he will teach sinners His ways. That is what David is doing in Psalm 32—instructing. So Psalm 32 is not a penitential psalm, but one of instruction.

Blessed is he whose transgression is forgiven, whose sin is covered [Ps. 32:1].

David is giving instruction here. He is telling us that he had made his confession to God, was forgiven, and had found complete restoration. He found shelter in God and was given a song of deliverance.

The word *blessed* in this verse means "happy." We have seen this word before in Psalm 1: "Blessed is the man that walketh not in the counsel of the ungodly, nor standeth in the way of sinners, nor sitteth in the seat of the scornful" (Ps. 1:1). The blessedness in Psalm 1 is that which only a perfect man can enjoy. I don't know about you, but I am not perfect. Psalm 1 actually speaks of the Lord Jesus who was the perfect man. "Blessed is the man that walketh not . . . that standeth not . . . and that sitteth not" (Paraphrase mine). That tells what the perfect man does not do. "But his delight is in the law of the Lord . . ." (v. 2). That Law condemns us. It did not condemn the Lord Jesus Christ. The law written in commandments and ordinances cannot give man blessedness. It demands a perfect obedience which man cannot attain, and thus it pronounces a curse on him. Galatians 3:10 tells us, "For as many as are of the works of the law are under the curse: for it is written, Cursed is every one that continueth not in all things which are written in the book of the law to do them." There is no man who can honestly say that he measures up to God's Law. If you can say that you measure up to the Law, then you can ask the Lord Jesus to move over from the right hand of God because that is your seat—you are perfect. Friend, neither you nor I are perfect, but the Lord Jesus Christ is perfect.

In Psalm 32:1 it is the blessedness of a man whose sin has been forgiven. Christ died for our sins; and, in His death as substitute for sinners, He met and satisfied the righteousness of God. So now the holy God can be a just God and a Savior—He can be just and the justifier of all those who believe in Jesus. When faith is exercised in Christ, it is counted for righteousness. In Romans 4:5 we read, "But to him that worketh not, but believeth on him that justifieth the ungodly, his faith is counted for righteousness." In this way thousands of Old Testament believers, beginning with Adam and Eve who looked for the Seed of the woman, were saved in anticipation of the finished work of the Lord Jesus Christ. David is expressing the blessedness, the happiness of a man whose sins had been forgiven.

Blessed is the man unto whom the LORD imputeth not iniquity, and in whose spirit there is no guile [Ps. 32:2].

God does not impute sin (or make sin over to the sinner) who trusts in Christ. That sin was put on Christ, "Who was delivered for our offences, and was raised again for our justification" (Rom. 4:25). "He knew no sin, but was made sin for us, that we might be made the righteousness of God in him" (2 Cor. 5:17, Paraphrase mine). What a wonderful thing God has done for us in Christ!

David relates his experience in trying to hide his sin.

When I kept silence, my bones waxed old through my roaring all the day long [Ps. 32:3].

He had sat on the throne, looked around at the crowd, and said, "Nobody here knows what I have done. Nobody knows about my sin. I have hidden it pretty well." But David's conscience bothered him. In fact, this verse tells us that even his bones bothered him. He began to lose weight, and his friends around him became uneasy. They felt that he needed to see a doctor—that he was probably suffering from some serious disease. But he just kept going through this agony from day to day.

For day and night thy hand was heavy upon me: my moisture is turned into the drought of summer. Selah [Ps. 32:4].

If you are a child of God, you can sin, but you cannot get by with it. That is the difference between the saved and the unsaved man. If you are a man of the world, you can get by with your sin temporarily, but a child of God cannot. The hand of God was heavy upon David day and night. Paul says, "For if we would judge ourselves, we should not be judged. But when we are judged, we are chastened of the Lord, that we should not be condemned with the world" (1 Cor. 11:31–32). If we do not judge ourselves, then God is going to judge us. God takes His own child to the woodshed for punishment.

Sometime after David's sin, the prophet Nathan came to David to reprove him, and he said, "David, I have a little story to tell you." This is the story: ". . . There were two men in one city; the one rich, and the other poor. The rich man had exceeding many flocks and herds: But the poor man had nothing, save one little ewe lamb, which he had bought and nourished up: and it grew up together with him, and with his children; it did eat of his own meat, and drank of his own cup, and lay in his bosom, and was unto him as a daughter. And there came a traveller unto the rich man, and he spared to take of his own flock and of his own herd, to dress for the wayfaring man that was come unto him; but took the poor man's lamb, and dressed it for the man that was come to him. And David's anger was greatly kindled against the man; and he said to Nathan, As the LORD liveth, the man that hath done this thing shall surely die: And he shall restore the lamb fourfold, because he did this thing, and because he had no pity. And Nathan said to David, Thou art the man . . ." (2 Sam. 12:1–7). Then David confessed his sin.

> **I acknowledged my sin unto thee, and mine iniquity have I not hid. I said, I will confess my transgressions unto the LORD; and thou forgavest the iniquity of my sin. Selah [Ps. 32:5].**

This is good instruction for you and me, is it not? If you are out of fellowship with God today, David in this verse tells about the way back. "If we confess our sins, he is faithful and just to forgive us our sins, and to cleanse us from all unrighteousness" (1 John 1:9).

> **For this shall every one that is godly pray unto thee in a time when thou mayest be found: surely in the floods of great waters they shall not come nigh unto him [Ps. 32:6].**

When David refers to the "floods of great waters," I think he is referring to the flood of Noah's time. Noah was in the ark when the Flood came, and that flood which destroyed others simply lifted him up because he was in the ark. The waters of judgment could not reach Noah. There is going to be another time of great judgment coming upon the earth, but it will not be a flood of water; it will be fire. What can you do at a time like that?

> **Thou art my hiding place; thou shalt preserve me from trouble; thou shalt compass me about with songs of deliverance. Selah [Ps. 32:7].**

This verse ends with the word *Selah*, which means "to stop, look, and listen." Think over what has been said. Selah is a musical rest, and I have a notion the orchestra did not play at this time, nor did the chorus sing. It was a time of silence so you could think over what had been sung. Think it over, friend. Have you lost fellowship with God? Do you need a hiding place? Well, God can be your hiding place.

> **I will instruct thee and teach thee in the way which thou shalt go: I will guide thee with mine eye [Ps. 32:8].**

You have to be very close to the Lord if you are going to be guided with His eye.

Now God uses a humorous comparison.

> **Be ye not as the horse, or as the mule, which have no understanding: whose mouth must be held in with bit and bridle, lest they come near unto thee [Ps. 32:9].**

There are many Christians who do not orbit in the will of God. They are way up in space; yet God will guide them by His overruling providence, as we learn in the little Book of Esther. He compares a believer who will not be led by God to an old hard-headed mule. It reminds me of the man in Texas who visited his friend who owned a little donkey. They hitched it to the wagon intending to take a ride and visit some mutual friends. Before they got in the wagon, the owner reached into the wagon, took out a two-by-four, and hit the donkey over the head. The man asked his friend, "Why in the world did you do that?" His friend replied, "I do that to get his attention." Many of us are like that donkey. That is why Scripture says, "Be ye not as the horse or as the mule, which have no understanding: whose mouth must be held in with bit and bridle."

This psalm closes on a high note.

> **Many sorrows shall be to the wicked: but he that trusteth in the LORD, mercy shall compass him about.**
>
> **Be glad in the LORD, and rejoice, ye righteous: and shout for joy, all ye that are upright in heart [Ps. 32:10–11].**

Whoever you are and wherever you are, if you know the Lord Jesus Christ as your Savior, you can lift up your heart in great joy to God.

PSALM 33

THEME: *A song of praise from a redeemed people*

In this psalm we find the praises of redeemed people. God is worshiped as the Creator and as providential Ruler. He is praised for His majestic and matchless grace. For the first time musical instruments are plainly mentioned in the text itself. This is one of the orphanic (orphan) psalms because the author's name is not given. It is one in this segment of psalms that David may not have written.

> **Rejoice in the LORD, O ye righteous: for praise is comely for the upright [Ps. 33:1].**

We are to rejoice in the presence of God. This is a beautiful psalm of praise. It sounds like David, and it is possible that he could have written it.

> **Praise the LORD with harp: sing unto him with the psaltery and an instrument of ten strings [Ps. 33:2].**

The psaltery is a stringed instrument resembling a zither.

> **Sing unto him a new song: play skilfully with a loud noise [Ps. 33:3].**

We are to sing a new song unto the Lord. What is that new song? Several psalms speak of a new song that will be sung in the future. I think when the time comes to sing that new song there will be new singers also. I am going to have a new body, and I think I will be able to sing. I hope the Lord will let me sing in heaven. Revelation 5:9 says, "And they sung a new song, saying, Thou art worthy to take the book, and to open the seals thereof: for thou wast slain, and hast redeemed us to

God by thy blood out of every kindred, and tongue, and people, and nation." The psalmist exhorts us to sing a song of praise to God because He is our *Creator*, but the new song we will sing in heaven will be because the Lord Jesus Christ is our *Redeemer*. In Revelation 14:3 we read, "And they sung as it were a new song before the throne, and before the four beasts, and the elders: and no man could learn that song but the hundred and forty and four thousand, which were redeemed from the earth." A new song will be sung in the future.

In this verse we are also told that we are to "play *skilfully*." Friend, I believe that if you are going to sing before a group of people you should sing well. Church music is in a sad state today. I visit many churches and hear many people sing who do not have a gift for singing. You may not be a trained musician, but you should be dead sure that you can sing and that your voice is a gift of the Spirit which He can use for the profit and building up of the church. Otherwise your effort will be an exercise in futility. And don't try to hit a high "C" when you cannot even hit a high "A" or "B"—that is an exercise in futility also!

For the word of the LORD is right; and all his works are done in truth [Ps. 33:4].

Notice the *Word* of God and the *works* of God, meaning His creative works.

By the word of the LORD were the heavens made; and all the host of them by the breath of his mouth [Ps. 33:6].

The Word of God is powerful! I once saw a demonstration by a singer who broke two or three glasses by hitting a high note. God used *His* voice to create, not destroy. He brought the universe into existence by His word. He said, ". . . Let there be light: and there was light" (Gen. 1:3). There is power in light, electrical power and electronic power. Do you realize that all of that came into existence when God spoke? God *spoke* into existence all created things. Vegetation, animal life, and man were all created by God's word. What tremendous power there is in His Word! I don't know *how* He did it, but I do know that God did it, and that is the important thing.

> **The LORD bringeth the counsel of the heathen to nought: he maketh the devices of the people of none effect [Ps. 33:10].**

The United Nations has selected to put up a verse like Isaiah 2:4 which says in part, ". . . and they shall beat their swords into plowshares, and their spears into pruninghooks: nation shall not lift up sword against nation, neither shall they learn war any more." They have used the wrong verse because it doesn't look to me like they are doing much beating—they are beating each other but not swords into plowshares. Instead, Psalm 33:10 should be written over the United Nations: "The LORD bringeth the counsel of the heathen [nations] to nought." That would be appropriate. Witness the past: the League of Nations, and before that, the Hague Conference on Peace, all came to naught. Do you know something else? I know I will be criticized for saying this, but the United Nations is also going to come to naught, because they have left God out.

> **Blessed is the nation whose God is the LORD; and the people whom he hath chosen for his own inheritance [Ps. 33:12].**

This is a verse I would love to put up in Washington so that the president and all of Congress could see it.

> **The LORD looketh from heaven; he beholdeth all the sons of men [Ps. 33:13].**

God sees the United Nations. He sees the president of the United States. He sees the Congress. He sees you. He sees me. No one escapes His eye.

**There is no king saved by the multitude of an host: a
mighty man is not delivered by much strength [Ps.
33:16].**

Napoleon said that God is on the side of the greatest battalion, but he
demonstrated he was wrong, because at the Battle of Waterloo Napoleon had the greatest battalion and lost. God is not on the side of the
one who has the biggest bomb, either.

**Behold, the eye of the LORD is upon them that fear him,
upon them that hope in his mercy [Ps. 33:18].**

How wonderful this is!

**For our heart shall rejoice in him, because we have
trusted in his holy name [Ps. 33:21].**

When we trust in the name of God, our hearts will rejoice. May I make
a suggestion? Why don't you saturate yourself with the Psalms? Instead of running around attending all of the conferences which tell
you about new methods of running Sunday school, running the
church, or doing this or that, why don't you stay home and read the
Psalms? When you are saturated with this portion of God's Word, it
not only will bring comfort to your heart, it will solve 99.4 percent of
the problems of the church. Oh, that it might become meaningful to
you personally and be translated into shoe leather! This is a rich area
of the Word of God.

PSALM 34

THEME: A song of praise for deliverance

This psalm has an explanation, which is part of the inspired text: "A Psalm of David, when he changed his behaviour before Abimelech; who drove him away, and he departed." This provides me with a fine opportunity to illustrate something that the critic has used to discredit the Word of God, which has led many uninstructed folks away from believing in the integrity and the inerrancy of Scripture. The occasion for this psalm goes back to an incident that is recorded in the life of David. You will recall that King Saul was after David. This young man was fleeing for his life and hiding in one cave after another. He was in that region of wilderness down toward the Dead Sea, and not many people can survive in that area. I have been driven through it, but I would not want to drive through it alone. David was able to survive in that wilderness, but he did grow weary; and his faith got very weak. He thought he was going to be destroyed, so he went west to the land of the Philistines. The king of the Philistines received David at that time, but some of his men distrusted him. "And the servants of Achish said unto him, Is not this David the king of the land? did they not sing one to another of him in dances, saying, Saul hath slain his thousands, and David his ten thousands? And David laid up these words in his heart, and was sore afraid of Achish the king of Gath" (1 Sam. 21:11–12). David realized that he was in real danger there in enemy territory, so he acted like an insane man. The king was disgusted at having an insane man in his presence, and he sent him away. So David's life was spared at this time. When David escaped and returned to the wilderness of Israel to hide, I think he was lying there in the safety of a cave, thinking, *I should have trusted God.*

Now if you turn back to 1 Samuel 21 and read the record, you will note that the king of Gath is called Achish, and in Psalm 34 he is called Abimelech. The critic sees this and says that it is quite obvious this is not an inspired psalm of David, and that this is an error in the Bible. The problem with the critic is that he looks only where he wants to look. Abimelech is a general title of royalty, just as Pharaoh was a general title in Egypt.

When I was teaching in a Bible institute a young fellow brought this problem of Achish and Abimelech to me. He said he believed in the inspiration of the Scriptures, but this was obviously an error, and he was greatly distressed by it. Of course, it was simply a lack of knowledge on his part. Remember, when you think you find an error in the Bible, the problem is not with the Bible but with you. That is the problem the critics have today.

As we consider this psalm, think of it in the light of David's experience.

> **I will bless the Lord at all times: his praise shall continually be in my mouth [Ps. 34:1].**

When you are in trouble, do you feel discouraged and defeated? David did. He kept running, running, running, and it looked like it would never come to an end. He lost heart and was discouraged. He thought, *One of these days I will be killed.* Yet he says, "I will bless the Lord at all times." My friend, I do pretty well in praising the Lord on a good sunshiny day and when things go right, but it is not so easy when things become difficult. Yet David could say, "His praise shall continually be in my mouth."

> **My soul shall make her boast in the Lord: the humble shall hear thereof, and be glad [Ps. 34:2].**

David's attitude was a testimony for the Lord.

> **O magnify the Lord with me, and let us exalt his name together [Ps. 34:3].**

I have thought about putting this verse on the letterhead we use at our *Thru the Bible Radio* headquarters. I want you to join with me in magnifying the Lord. We are going to find out in one of the psalms that the *Word* of God and the *name* of God are just about the same. Both are important. We want to get out the Word of God because it will magnify the name of the Lord. I would like to say with the psalmist, O magnify the Lord with me, and let us exalt His name together, in getting out the Word of God today.

The first three verses are sheer praise to God; they are the Hallelujah Chorus. Now he gives us the reason for his praise.

> **I sought the Lord, and he heard me, and delivered me from all my fears [Ps. 34:4].**

How wonderful!

> **They looked unto him, and were lightened: and their faces were not ashamed.**

> **This poor man cried, and the Lord heard him, and saved him out of all his troubles [Ps. 34:5-6].**

How thankful David was for God's deliverance. And, friend, I thank God for the way He has led me. I am sure you do, too.

> **The angel of the Lord encampeth round about them that fear him, and delivereth them [Ps. 34:7].**

The Angel of the Lord is mentioned only three times in the Psalms. He is mentioned in Psalm 34:7 and in Psalm 35:5-6 and that is all. I am not going to go into any detail about this subject, but I believe the Angel of the Lord is the preincarnate Christ. You do not find the Angel of the Lord in the New Testament because the Lord is no longer an angel, but a Man. When He appeared in the Old Testament as an angel, He was none other than the Lord Jesus Christ. In this verse the psalmist tells us that the "angel of the LORD encampeth round about them that fear him, and delivereth them." In Hebrews 13:5 the Lord Jesus says, ". . . I will never leave thee, nor forsake thee." In Matthew 28:20 the Lord says, ". . . lo, I am with you alway, even unto the end of the world. Amen."

Now David extends an invitation:

**O taste and see that the LORD is good: blessed is the man
that trusteth in him [Ps. 34:8].**

David says, "If you don't believe what I have said is true, taste for yourself and see that the Lord is good." Blessed or *happy* is the man who trusts in the Lord. There is nothing like it.

David had been hunted by Saul for a long time. He had hidden in caves and had become a rugged outdoorsman. He had seen the sight mentioned in the following verse.

**The young lions do lack, and suffer hunger: but they that
seek the LORD shall not want any good thing [Ps. 34:10].**

David had seen hungry little lion cubs whining for something to eat. He also had seen that those who had sought the Lord had not lacked any good thing. If a lioness can take care of her little cubs, God can take care of you and me. David learned that by experience. This is putting Christianity into shoe leather, and we need it in shoe leather. I am tired of Sunday morning Christianity. People come to church, sing a few hymns, listen to the sermon, and sing the Doxology. That just about ends it for many folks. I love what a broker in San Francisco wrote—it was one of the nicest things anyone had said: "You do not sound like you are speaking behind a stained glass window." I thank God for that. There is nothing wrong with speaking behind stained glass windows—I did that for forty years—but I would rather it sounded as if it came from the marketplace, the schoolroom, the office, and the workshop. David had experienced God's care. He knew it was real.

Keep thy tongue from evil, and thy lips from speaking guile [Ps. 34:13].

This is something that I need to learn. Perhaps you also need to learn it.

The eyes of the LORD are upon the righteous, and his ears are open unto their cry [Ps. 34:15].

God hears and answers prayer. It may not be the answer we were expecting, because sometimes He says no.

The face of the LORD is against them that do evil, to cut off the remembrance of them from the earth [Ps. 34:16].

There is a lot of sentimental rot today in dramatic productions of some old low-down sinner who deserts his wife and baby so he can live a life of sin. Maybe he becomes a thief or a murderer, but one day he comes home and finds his little child sick. He gets down by the side of the bed and prays. This kind of story brings boo-hoos all over the audience. I don't know about you, but it turns my tummy. Do you know why? God says, "I don't hear the prayer of a man like that." Such a person has no right to go to God and ask Him for anything except salvation. You don't even have to ask for forgiveness. He's got forgiveness for you. All you have to do is confess yourself a sinner and trust Christ as your Savior. He will automatically forgive you. ". . . Believe on the Lord Jesus Christ, and thou shalt be saved . . ." (Acts 16:31).

The LORD is nigh unto them that are of a broken heart; and saveth such as be of a contrite spirit [Ps. 34:18].

If a person is willing to take the place of humility, come to the Lord as a sinner and trust Him, the Lord will be near to him. Now if that old reprobate who got down by the bed and prayed for his sick child will acknowledge his sin and accept Jesus Christ as his Savior, then God will hear his prayer for his child. The Lord is near those who have a broken heart.

Many are the afflictions of the righteous: but the LORD delivereth him out of them all [Ps. 34:19].

No one is free from trouble—regardless of who he is. But when we are God's children we can expect God's deliverance. Oh, how good He is. Let's bless Him at all times, even as David did.

PSALM 35

THEME: A plea for deliverance from his enemies

This is a psalm that David wrote during the days of the persecution by King Saul. First Samuel 24 probably contains the background for this psalm. It is David's powerful appeal to a righteous God to execute judgment upon the enemies of God and the persecutors of His righteous people.

There are folk who say that this is not the kind of prayer a Christian should pray and that the Lord Jesus did not talk like this. However, the Lord Jesus did give a parable about a widow who went to a judge saying, "Avenge me of mine adversary." That judge took a long time to do it, but he finally saw that the widow got justice. It is a parable by contrast. God is not an unfeeling, hardheaded judge. God is gracious, wonderful, and eager to help His children, and we are to turn over to Him our grievances. And Paul gives believers this admonition: "Dearly beloved, avenge not yourselves, but rather give place unto wrath: for it is written, Vengeance is mine; I will repay, saith the Lord" (Rom. 12:19). You and I are not to take vengeance. We are to turn that over to God—it is His department. He will handle it better than either you or I will handle it.

I want to speak quite frankly. I have turned several people over to the Lord when what I wanted to do was smack them in the mouth. There is no use beating around the bush—I have that feeling sometimes. I know a man who is a liar; yet he pretends to be an outstanding Christian and carries a big Bible under his arm! God told me, "Vernon, don't hit him in the mouth. That would be wrong—you wouldn't be walking by faith. You trust Me. Vengeance is mine. I will repay." So I turned that man over to the Lord. I think the Lord will spank him. We need to learn to walk the pathway of faith.

When David wrote this psalm, he was in trouble. He was running away from Saul. Yet when David had an opportunity to kill Saul, he refused to do it. Saul knew that David had spared his life, and in 1 Samuel 24 Saul even said to him that he knew God had given the kingdom to David and admitted that David was more righteous than he was. Yet he continued to treat David as an enemy instead of bringing him home in peace.

David's imprecatory prayer is not only personal but prophetic. David's persecution pictures the remnant of Israel during the Tribulation period. The cry for righteous judgment will be answered when the Lord Jesus Christ comes the second time. He will execute judgment and will deliver God's elect.

> **Let them be confounded and put to shame that seek after my soul: let them be turned back and brought to confusion that devise my hurt.**
>
> **Let them be as chaff before the wind: and let the angel of the LORD chase them [Ps. 35:4–5].**

David wanted to turn it over to the Lord, you see.

Here is the second mention of the "angel of the LORD"—the first was in Psalm 34:7. Again let me say that I believe the Angel of the Lord is none other than the preincarnate Christ. He is the deliverer and the executor of judgment.

> **Let their way be dark and slippery: and let the angel of the LORD persecute them.**
>
> **For without cause have they hid for me their net in a pit, which without cause they have digged for my soul.**
>
> **Let destruction come upon him at unawares; and let his net that he hath hid catch himself: into that very destruction let him fall [Ps. 35:6–8].**

This sounds extreme! It is an imprecatory prayer. I do think it is inconsistent for a Christian to pray a prayer like that today since God has told us to turn things over to Him. But if you think God is not going to

take vengeance on evildoers, you are mistaken. He will do it without
being vindictive. He will do it in justice and in righteousness and in
holiness. We do well in turning over to God our grievances because
He is going to make things right. This is a great psalm, a great comfort
and solace for the soul of man.

Now listen to David after he has prayed that prayer.

> **And my soul shall be joyful in the LORD: it shall rejoice
> in his salvation.**

> **All my bones shall say, LORD, who is like unto thee,
> which deliverest the poor from him that is too strong for
> him, yea, the poor and the needy from him that spoileth
> him? [Ps. 35:9–10].**

At this time in David's life he was a very poor man. While he was in
exile there came to him men who were in debt, men who were in distress, and men who were discontented. These were his companions,
and they shared his rugged existence and his poverty. But God was
with them, and He "delivered the poor from him that was too strong
for him."

> **With hypocritical mockers in feasts, they gnashed upon
> me with their teeth [Ps. 35:16].**

A mocker in that day was a court jester who was hired to amuse the
guests at a banquet. In this case they would make fun of David for
running away and hiding from Saul. They probably would say, "He
could slay the giant Goliath, but he is afraid of King Saul."

Hypocritical mockers are about us today, and you will find them in
the church. I was a pastor for a long time, and I have seen them. Since
I am no longer a pastor, I am in a position to say some things that need
to be said. Mockers hurt the testimony of the church. The church is
the bride of Christ; God still has a purpose for her, and somebody
needs to do some cleaning up on the inside. We are not to judge the
world, but we are to judge the things inside the church. There are

those who ridicule God's men, and they lie about God's men—doing it in a most pious way. They are hypocritical mockers. They are *jesters* in the court of God, ridiculing God's men.

My friend, it is good to know that although the righteous do suffer ridicule and even affliction, and although the enemy rejoices over their suffering, the end is always deliverance. In God's kingdom the righteous will have their share.

PSALM 36

THEME: A picture of the wicked

This psalm has the inscription of David as the "servant of Jehovah." The psalm gives us a view of the human heart, which is *wicked*. You may not believe this, but every human being has a wicked heart. Jeremiah 17:9 tells us, "The heart is deceitful above all things, and desperately wicked: who can know it?" Fortunately God has a remedy for heart trouble.

> **The transgression of the wicked saith within my heart, that there is no fear of God before his eyes [Ps. 36:1].**

The Septuagint translation, which is the Greek translation made by the seventy in Egypt, of this verse reads, "The wicked hath an oracle of transgression in his heart." What is that oracle of transgression in the heart? It is the old nature that everyone has, the Adamic nature. In Matthew 15:19 the Lord Jesus Christ says, "For out of the heart proceed evil thoughts, murders, adulteries, fornications, thefts, false witness, blasphemies." It's an ugly brood that comes out of the human heart.

"There is no fear of God before their eyes" is quoted by Paul in Romans 3:18. This is a revelation of the wicked. "The wicked hath an oracle of transgression in his heart." That old evil nature has a hold on mankind. To those who say, "Let your conscience be your guide," I want to say, "Your conscience is not your guide." The Holy Spirit is your guide. Your conscience is like a barometer that will let you know if what you have done is right or wrong. Let the Holy Spirit be your guide. Your conscience is that which will prick you after you have done something wrong.

> **For he flattereth himself in his own eyes, until his iniquity be found to be hateful [Ps. 36:2].**

Matthew Henry, in his commentary, makes a very interesting statement in this connection. He says that sinners are self-destroyed. "They are self-destroyers by being self-flatterers; Satan could not deceive them, if they did not deceive themselves. But will the cheat last always? No, the day is coming when the sinner will be undeceived, when his iniquity shall be found hateful." I think that one of the things the lost will have to live with throughout eternity is an old nature that he is going to learn to hate. That is the thing that will make his own little hell on the inside of his skin!

> **The words of his mouth are iniquity and deceit: he hath
> left off to be wise, and to do good [Ps. 36:3].**

On the golf course I met a man, a fine-looking man who had retired from an excellent position. All that came out of his mouth was iniquity. In every breath he uttered he took God's name in vain. "The words of his mouth are iniquity and deceit."

> **He deviseth mischief upon his bed; he setteth himself in
> a way that is not good; he abhorreth not evil [Ps. 36:4].**

In his bed he plans the evil he is going to do the next day. This is a frightful picture!

Now we have a picture of what God is:

> **Thy mercy, O Lord, is in the heavens; and thy faithfulness reacheth unto the clouds.**

> **Thy righteousness is like the great mountains; thy judgments are a great deep: O Lord, thou preservest man and beast.**

> **How excellent is thy lovingkindness, O God! therefore
> the children of men put their trust under the shadow of
> thy wings [Ps. 36:5-7].**

What blessed, wonderful words these are. This is the God that man rejects. This is the God whom men do not fear. The wicked do not know this God, and they have no idea what it is like to be under His wings. That is the place where the righteous take refuge. I like to talk about the wings of Jehovah. In Exodus 19:4 God told Israel, "Ye have seen what I did unto the Egyptians, and how I bare you on eagles' wings, and brought you unto myself." Under His wings there is protection, security, rest, and the warmth of God's love. Jesus said, "O Jerusalem, Jerusalem, thou that killest the prophets, and stonest them which are sent unto thee, how often would I have gathered thy children together, even as a hen gathereth her chickens under her wings, and ye would not!" (Matt. 23:37). This is the God that many people are rejecting today!

> **Let not the foot of pride come against me, and let not the hand of the wicked remove me.**
>
> **There are the workers of iniquity fallen: they are cast down, and shall not be able to rise [Ps. 36:11–12].**

David prays that God will continue giving His mercy and grace to him so that he will not fall under the hand of the wicked. This is something that every believer should pray. We live in a wicked, mean world. My prayer has always been, "Oh, God, don't let me fall into the hands of the wicked."

PSALM 37

THEME: A promise of future blessing

This is a psalm of David. It is an experience of David and a promise of future blessing to the remnant of Israel written in the form of an acrostic. Each verse in this psalm begins with a letter of the Hebrew alphabet. There are forty verses in Psalm 37, which means two verses would begin with each letter of the Hebrew alphabet. For example, two verses of this psalm begin with Aleph, two verses with Beth, two verses with Gimel, etc., right through the alphabet. That is the way we instruct our children. I still remember a book I got when I was a little fellow: "A is for apple, B is for baby, C is for cat," etc., with illustrating pictures for each. This psalm is constructed in a similar way. It has been a great blessing to God's people down through the years, although it is often misapplied.

> **Fret not thyself because of evildoers, neither be thou envious against the workers of iniquity.**
>
> **For they shall soon be cut down like the grass, and wither as the green herb [Ps. 37:1–2].**

The prosperity of evildoers troubled David a great deal. It is a subject that is dealt with in Psalm 73 and one that is presented elsewhere in the Old Testament. Why do the godless people seem to prosper? In the Old Testament, God promised believers *earthly* and *material* prosperity. He has not promised that to believers today. Our hope is in heaven, not on earth. But the hope of Israel was upon the earth. The man of that day looked about and saw the ungodly prosper. He could see the fields of the ungodly being watered by the rain and flourishing, while down the road a poor righteous man was having a hard time. It was difficult to understand the reason for this.

David came to the conclusion, as Asaph did in Psalm 73, that someday the wicked would be cut down just like the grass. A few years ago I had people in my congregation who could not understand why God would permit Hitler to do the things he was doing. Why, he almost won World War II. Why would God permit a man like Mussolini to do some of the things he did? But where are these men today? Just give God time. He will deal with the wicked. It is the *end* of the ungodly that we need to consider. If it disturbs you when you look around today and see the wicked prospering, there are several things you can do to solve your problem.

> **Trust in the LORD, and do good; so shalt thou dwell in the land, and verily thou shalt be fed [Ps. 37:3].**

This was a promise to God's earthly people. He told them, "Don't worry about the wicked. You trust in Me, and I will take care of you."

> **Delight thyself also in the LORD; and he shall give thee the desires of thine heart [Ps. 37:4].**

This was a promise for Israel, but it also applies to us today. I am not sure that He is going to bless your business, but He has already blessed you with spiritual blessings, and He will shower on you all of the spiritual blessings you can contain. Then notice what we are to do. We are to delight ourselves in the Lord.

Now, there is something else that we can do.

> **Commit thy way unto the LORD: trust also in him; and he shall bring it to pass [Ps. 37:5].**

"Commit thy way unto the LORD." Many Christians criticize and find fault with God—they have not committed their way to the Lord.

"Trust also in him; and he shall bring it to pass." Give God time. He will work things out in your life. God is *good,* my friend. The heathen concept of God is as a terrible Being. Their idols are hideous.

Many Christians view God that way. They think of Him as sort of a villain who will turn on you at any moment. He never will—He is your Friend. He loves you. He wants to save you, but you have to commit your way to Him.

> **Rest in the LORD, and wait patiently for him: fret not thyself because of him who prospereth in his way, because of the man who bringeth wicked devices to pass [Ps. 37:7].**

Here is another thing to do: "Rest in the LORD, and wait patiently for him." How wonderful it is. When the wicked prosper, don't fret. When the ungodly bring their wicked devices to pass, don't let it disturb you. Don't get "uptight" about it.

> **Cease from anger, and forsake wrath: fret not thyself in any wise to do evil [Ps. 37:8].**

"Cease from anger"—don't lose your temper.
    If you do evil, don't think you can get by with it. If you are God's child, you will find yourself in deep trouble if you try to get by with evil.

> **For evildoers shall be cut off: but those that wait upon the LORD, they shall inherit the earth [Ps. 37:9].**

God will see to it that those who wait upon the Lord will one day inherit the earth. The wicked are going to be cut off.

> **But the meek shall inherit the earth; and shall delight themselves in the abundance of peace [Ps. 37:11].**

Someday the meek shall inherit the earth. The day will come when God will put His people on the earth. I heard a preacher say, "God is going to save so many people that there won't be enough room for them on earth, so He made heaven to take care of the overflow." Heaven is not for the overflow; it is for the church. Israel will inherit the earth. To make a statement like that preacher did is to hopelessly confuse the purposes of God.

> **The wicked have drawn out the sword, and have bent their bow, to cast down the poor and needy, and to slay such as be of upright conversation [Ps. 37:14].**

The Scripture makes it clear that if you take the sword, that is the way you will perish.

> **A little that a righteous man hath is better than the riches of many wicked [Ps. 37:16].**

Having traveled a lot in the course of my ministry, I have been in the homes of very poor saints and also in the homes of some very rich saints. It has been my experience that the happiest saints are those who do not have so much. God seems to see to that.

> **But the wicked shall perish, and the enemies of the LORD shall be as the fat of lambs: they shall consume; into smoke shall they consume away [Ps. 37:20].**

The wicked are going to perish. Don't concern yourself with their prosperity. That is God's department, and He will take care of it.

> **The steps of a good man are ordered by the LORD: and he delighteth in his way [Ps. 37:23].**

"The steps of a good man are ordered by the LORD," that is, they are established by the Lord on a foundation that is the Rock—and the Rock is Christ.

"He delighteth in his way." Does God delight in you today? God could point to Job—who was not sinless by any means—but God took delight in him.

> **The righteous shall inherit the land, and dwell therein for ever [Ps. 37:29].**

This verse again tells us that God is going to make good His promise to Abraham and to the children of Israel. He promised them earthly blessings. He did not promise that to you and me. We are blessed with all spiritual blessings. You will be confused if you believe God has promised you earthly blessings. It is true that many Christians are blessed with material things, but that is surplus. It is an added blessing; and, if God has blessed you that way, you have a tremendous responsibility. I feel sorry for some of the rich saints who are not using their money the way God wants them to use it.

> **Mark the perfect man, and behold the upright: for the end of that man is peace.**

> **But the transgressors shall be destroyed together: the end of the wicked shall be cut off [Ps. 37:37–38].**

The "perfect man" is one who is perfect toward God in that he trusts God and rests upon his salvation. The end of the upright man is peace. God will see to that.

"The end of the wicked shall be cut off." The transgressors will be destroyed and the wicked shall be cut off. Mark that down. It is as sure as the law of gravitation.

PSALM 38

THEME: *A penitential psalm involving physical disease*

This is entitled "A Psalm of David, to bring to remembrance" and is classed as a penitential psalm. It is David's confession and concerns physical sickness. David is very ill. His body is wasting away. We have no record of his having this illness, but we have seen before that he thanked God for his healing.

> **O Lord, rebuke me not in thy wrath: neither chasten me in thy hot displeasure [Ps. 38:1].**

David, in deep distress, prays that God will not judge him in anger.

> **For thine arrows stick fast in me, and thy hand presseth me sore [Ps. 38:2].**

This is real conviction.

> **There is no soundness in my flesh because of thine anger; neither is there any rest in my bones because of my sin [Ps. 38:3].**

David's physical sickness is the result of sin.

> **For mine iniquities are gone over mine head: as an heavy burden they are too heavy for me [Ps. 38:4].**

You and I cannot carry our burdens, friend, and we especially cannot carry the burden of sin. We must give that burden to God.

My wounds stink and are corrupt because of my foolishness.

I am troubled; I am bowed down greatly; I go mourning all the day long.

For my loins are filled with a loathsome disease: and there is no soundness in my flesh.

I am feeble and sore broken: I have roared by reason of the disquietness of my heart [Ps. 38:5–8].

Disease, the result of his foolishness, is followed by mental anguish. In the first church in which I served, there was a doctor in the congregation. He called me into his office one day and showed me this psalm. He said, "There are many people who believe that David had a venereal disease. I was told that in medical school, but I do not agree with it." He asked me what I thought. Well, I agreed with him that I would not accept that diagnosis.

Regarding the prophetic aspect of this psalm, some have interpreted it as being a description of the condition of Christ on the cross, that when Christ bore our sins, He also bore our diseases and actually took in His own body all the diseases of mankind.

This could not be true, because disease is the result of sin, and there was no sin in Him. Concerning His birth, Luke 1:35 says, "And the angel answered and said unto her, The Holy Ghost shall come upon thee, and the power of the Highest shall overshadow thee: therefore also that *holy* thing which shall be born of thee shall be called the Son of God." He was holy—He was not born with a sin nature. Of Christ's earthly life the Father said, ". . . Thou art my beloved Son, in whom I am well pleased" (Mark 1:11). Toward the end of His life on earth the Lord Jesus said, "Which of you convinceth me of sin? . . ." (John 8:46). Jesus was holy, harmless, and separate from sin. He could not be the spotless Lamb offered for our sin if He were diseased—disease is the result of sin.

Christ was holy when He went to the cross. For the first three hours that Christ was on the cross, man did his worst; but in those last three hours God did His best, for Christ took upon Himself the sin of the world. It is at this point that we need to be careful. It was the sin of the world that Christ took. When we are told that He bore our diseases, it is the disease of sin. Simon Peter confirms this in 1 Peter 2:24: "Who his own self bare our sins in his own body on the tree, that we, being dead to sins, should live unto righteousness: by whose stripes ye were healed"—healed of what? Our diseases? No! We are healed of sin. He bore our sins on the cross and took care of the sin problem for us. He did not have a diseased body. Disease is the result of sin, and there was no sin in the Lord Jesus Christ. It is an awful, blasphemous thing to say that Jesus Christ was diseased when He hung on the cross.

Those of us who have endured illness and disease in our bodies can identify with David in this psalm. And it is the proper thing to do to first take your case to the Great Physician—and then make an appointment with the best doctor you can find. Let's be practical about this. All the skill and wisdom a doctor has comes from God, whether or not he acknowledges it.

PSALM 39

THEME: *A psalm for funerals*

This remarkable psalm reveals to us the frailty, weakness, and the littleness of humanity. It sets before us the vanity of human existence. This psalm has been used at funerals a great deal, and it can be used so properly. There are those who have considered it probably "the most beautiful of all elegies in the Psalter." Dean Perowne has said: "The holy singer had long pent up his feelings; and though busy thoughts were stirring within him, he would not give them utterance. He could not bare his bosom to the rude gaze of an unsympathizing world. And he feared lest, while telling his perplexities, some word might drop from his lips which would give the wicked an occasion to speak evil against God. And when at last, unable to repress his strong emotion, he speaks to God and not to man, it is as one who feels how hopeless the problem of life is, except as seen in the light of God" (*The Book of Psalms*, p. 295). He speaks of this frailty and sinfulness, this weakness and littleness of mankind, with deep conviction. Candidly, human life is, without a doubt, the most colossal failure in God's universe. Apart from a relationship with God, my friend, it is rather meaningless. All is vanity—that is what you have to say under the sun. Without the Son of God it means nothing at all.

This is a psalm of David, and it is dedicated "To the chief Musician, even to Jeduthun." Who is Jeduthun? Perhaps he wrote the music for this psalm. He was one of three musical or choir directors connected with Israel's worship. Asaph and Heman were the other two men. David, the sweet singer of Israel, had associated himself with these three men in the ministry of music.

Now notice the beautiful words of this psalm.

> **I said, I will take heed to my ways, that I sin not with my tongue: I will keep my mouth with a bridle, while the wicked is before me [Ps. 39:1].**

This psalm concerns a subject that David would rather not talk about with the man of the world. "He would not quite understand it, so I put a zipper on my mouth."

I was dumb with silence, I held my peace, even from good; and my sorrow was stirred [Ps. 39:2].

But David wanted to say something, and finally he opens his heart before God.

My heart was hot within me, while I was musing the fire burned: then spake I with my tongue [Ps. 39:3].

He speaks now to the Lord:

LORD, make me to know mine end, and the measure of my days, what it is; that I may know how frail I am [Ps. 39:4].

David recognizes the frailty of man and asks, "What is the purpose of life? What is it that gives meaning to existence?" This is a current question being asked by young people today and they are asking it with a bang. After World War II my generation wanted to settle down in peace. We wanted a nice little bungalow, one or two cars in the garage, and a chicken in the pot. We wanted to live in an affluent society and shut our eyes to everything else in order to escape responsibility. Things did not turn out the way we wanted them to. We got tied up in traffic snarls. Our lives became filled with tension. The young generation came along (even those who came from Christian homes), looked around and asked "Is this what life is all about? What is the meaning of life?" This was David's question.

Christians can live in such a way today that there is no meaning to life. If you are a Christian parent, are you living a life that is turning your children *on* to Jesus Christ, or are you turning them *off* to everything that is Christian? There are many vagrants drifting over the face of the earth who have left home and gotten into a lot of trouble because of the poor examples set before them. Many of them have come from "good homes"—from all outward appearances they were good homes—but these young folk looked at the lives of their parents and said, "They have no meaning."

Oh, this psalm is relevant to the contemporary generation. David prayed, "LORD, make me to know mine end, and the measure of my days, what it is"—give me purpose and meaning.

Behold, thou hast made my days as an handbreadth; and mine age is as nothing before thee: verily every man at his best state is altogether vanity. Selah [Ps. 39:5].

This verse ends with the word *Selah*—stop, look, and listen; think this over, friend. The brevity of human life on this earth ought to tell us something. If this life is all there is to human existence, it is a colossal failure. I would rather be a dinosaur or a redwood tree and hang around for awhile, because compared to them man's life is just a handbreadth.

Surely every man walketh in a vain shew: surely they are disquieted in vain: he heapeth up riches, and knoweth not who shall gather them [Ps. 39:6].

William Thackeray, an English novelist and a Christian, wrote a novel called *Vanity Fair*. I enjoyed that book. It is a brilliant satire on a little group of people, a clique that had its status symbols, played its little parts, and committed its little sins that are an awful stench in heaven. They lived and died with their littleness and their bickerings. That's life! "Surely every man walketh in a vain shew . . . he heapeth up riches, and knoweth not who shall gather them." Nothing has changed. Think of the Christians who gather fortunes down here and leave it for godless offspring, or they leave it to unworthy so-called Christian work. We see a great deal of this. The psalmist saw it and asked, "What is the purpose of it all?"

And now, Lord, what wait I for? my hope is in thee [Ps. 39:7].

David turned to God—"my hope is in thee." Friend, if you don't turn to God, you will not find the meaning of life.

Deliver me from all my transgressions: make me not the reproach of the foolish [Ps. 39:8].

David wanted to be a good example.

I was dumb, I opened not my mouth; because thou didst it [Ps. 39:9].

He did not want to express his thoughts to the crowd, because they are rather pessimistic.

Remove thy stroke away from me: I am consumed by the blow of thine hand [Ps. 39:10].

He was feeling the discipline of God in his life—and it was for a purpose. Oh, my friend, how we need to get a proper perspective of life! The grave is not its goal. Longfellow wrote, "Dust thou art, to dust returnest, was not spoken of the soul." Man is going on a long journey. Eternity is ahead. What glorious anticipation there should be!

Hear my prayer, O Lord, and give ear unto my cry; hold not thy peace at my tears: for I am a stranger with thee, and a sojourner, as all my fathers were [Ps. 39:12].

We are just pilgrims and strangers down here, but we don't think of it that way. We want to fix up our little corner of the earth and think it is going to be permanent. We want to wrap ourselves in a blanket of false security. May I say, at best we are pilgrims and strangers on earth, and that is the way we ought to live our lives. We are on a journey, and we seek a city ". . . whose builder and maker is God" (Heb. 11:10). Oh, to have a hope today! The psalmist says of God, "My hope is in thee."

> **O spare me, that I may recover strength, before I go hence, and be no more [Ps. 39:13].**

That is, enable me to so live that my life will cause men and women to think on eternity. Enable me to live a life that will not turn folk away from God but draw them to Him. We hear a lot today about personal witnessing, but what about the testimony of our lives? Are people turning to God because of the way we are living, or are they turning away from God? I am confident that our lives are doing one or the other.

PSALM 40

THEME: *A messianic psalm predicting the crucifixion of Christ*

Two messianic psalms, 40 and 41, conclude the Genesis section of the Psalms. They are called messianic psalms because they are so quoted in the New Testament, which makes them especially important.

> **I waited patiently for the Lord; and he inclined unto me, and heard my cry [Ps. 40:1].**

This is a proper psalm to follow Psalm 39. All of these psalms go together; that is, you will note a continuity. There are those who feel that this psalm expresses the experience of David in his flight from Absalom, and that is accurate to a point. But this psalm is quoted in the Epistle to the Hebrews in a most remarkable way. In this psalm the One who celebrates in praise and thanksgiving the Resurrection, the triumph and Ascension is the Lord Jesus Himself. This is truly a messianic psalm. It reveals that the death of Christ was not a defeat at all. It was a great victory. When He says, "I waited patiently for the Lord; and he inclined unto me, and heard my cry," He is referring to His cry from the cross.

> **He brought me up also out of an horrible pit, out of the miry clay, and set my feet upon a rock, and established my goings [Ps. 40:2].**

Christ's agony and death is likened to a horrible pit, a pit of destruction. We cannot conceive how terrible the death of Christ on the cross really was.

> **And he hath put a new song in my mouth, even praise unto our God: many shall see it, and fear, and shall trust in the LORD [Ps. 40:3].**

This verse mentions a new song—we have read about a new song before—it is the song of redemption.

"Many shall see it, and fear, and shall trust in the LORD." What are they going to see? They will see the death and resurrection of the Lord Jesus Christ.

> **Blessed is that man that maketh the LORD his trust, and respecteth not the proud, nor such as turn aside to lies [Ps. 40:4].**

Our Lord Jesus Christ is the example of a man who puts his trust in God, who does not respect the proud, and who does not turn aside to lies.

> **Many, O LORD my God, are thy wonderful works which thou hast done, and thy thoughts which are to us-ward: they cannot be reckoned up in order unto thee: if I would declare and speak of them, they are more than can be numbered [Ps. 40:5].**

God has revealed what He thinks of us by sending His Son to die on the cross. At the time I am writing this, I often hear speculations as to the possibility of life on planets other than our own. I am certainly no expert in this field, but I think it may be possible that other planets are inhabited. But I can guarantee this: there will not be a cross on any of the planets out there in space. It was only here that the Son of God died on a cross. How wonderful! "Many, O LORD my God, are thy wonderful works which thou hast done, and thy thoughts which are toward us." My, how the Cross reveals God's love for us!

Now the following is quoted in the Epistle to the Hebrews:

Sacrifice and offering thou didst not desire; mine ears hast thou opened: burnt offering and sin offering hast thou not required.

Then said I, Lo, I come: in the volume of the book it is written of me,

I delight to do thy will, O my God: yea, thy law is within my heart.

I have preached righteousness in the great congregation: lo, I have not refrained my lips, O LORD, thou knowest [Ps. 40:6–9].

This is a marvelous psalm that follows the preceding one which reveals the frailty of man.

"Sacrifice and offering thou didst not desire; mine ears hast thou opened." Now notice how this is quoted in Hebrews 10:5, "Wherefore when he cometh into the world, he saith, Sacrifice and offering thou wouldest not, but a body hast thou prepared me." Now, wait a minute. Is this misquoted? Critics of the Bible say, "Oh, here is an error, a contradiction in the Bible. In Psalm 40:6 it says '. . . mine ears hast thou opened . . .'; and in Hebrews it says, '. . . a body hast thou prepared me.'"

The Holy Spirit is the author of the Bible. He wrote the Old Testament and the New Testament. He wrote both Psalms and Hebrews, and He has a perfect right to change His own writing. When He does, there is always a good reason.

Now let's consider the background. In Exodus 21 there is a law concerning servants and masters. If a man became a slave to another man, at the end of a certain period of time he could go free. Suppose during that period he met another slave, a woman, they fell in love and married and had children. When it was time for the man to go free, he could leave, but his wife and children could not go with him because she was a slave. What could this man do? He could decide that because he loved his master and his wife he would not leave.

"Then his master shall bring him unto the judges; he shall also bring him to the door, or unto the door post; and his master shall bore his ear through with an awl; and he shall serve him for ever" (Exod. 21:6).

The psalmist is referring to this custom when he says, "mine ears hast thou opened." When the Lord Jesus came to this earth, did He have His ear thrust through with an awl? No, He was given a body. He took upon Himself our humanity. He identified Himself with us and He became a servant. And He became a sacrifice. "Sacrifice and offering thou didst not desire"—God did not delight in all the animal offerings in the Old Testament, but they pointed to the sacrifice of the Lord Jesus Christ.

Now notice what Isaiah says on this subject. "The Lord GOD hath opened mine ear, and I was not rebellious, neither turned away back" (Isa. 50:5). This verse is prophesying the humiliation of the Servant (Christ) who would come to earth. When the Lord Jesus came down to this earth and went to the cross, His ear wasn't "opened" or "digged"; He was given a body, and that body was nailed to a cross. My friend, He has taken a glorified body with nail prints in it back to heaven, and He will bear those nail prints and scars throughout eternity that you and I might be presented without spot or blemish before Him. You see, He did more than have His ear bored through with an awl; He gave His body to be crucified because He loved us and would not return to heaven without us.

My friend, this is a marvelous messianic psalm that reveals the crucifixion of the Lord Jesus Christ because He loved us.

PSALM 41

THEME: *A messianic psalm predicting the betrayal of Judas*

This messianic psalm was written by David probably at the time he was betrayed by Ahithophel, his trusted counselor. Ahithophel sided with David's son Absalom when he led a rebellion against his father. Finally Ahithophel committed suicide by hanging himself (2 Sam. 17:23). Ahithophel foreshadows the betrayer of Christ, Judas Iscariot, and is so quoted by our Lord Himself.

This psalm opens with a blessing.

> **Blessed is he that considereth the poor: the LORD will deliver him in time of trouble [Ps. 41:1].**

It opens with "blessed" and closes with "blessed." It begins with, "Blessed is he that considereth the poor," and ends with, "Blessed be the LORD God of Israel." The word *blessed* as we have already seen, means "happy," so that the Genesis section of the Psalms (Psalms 1—41) begins with "happy" and closes with "happy."

Now notice the section that makes this a messianic psalm:

> **Yea, mine own familiar friend, in whom I trusted, which did eat of my bread, hath lifted up his heel against me [Ps. 41:9].**

Jesus quoted this verse in reference to Judas, "I speak not of you all: I know whom I have chosen: but that the scripture may be fulfilled, He that eateth bread with me hath lifted up his heel against me" (John 13:18). This verse was fulfilled in Judas, the one who betrayed the Lord Jesus. Peter also referred to it in Acts 1:16, "Men and brethren, this scripture must needs have been fulfilled, which the Holy Ghost by the mouth of David spake before concerning Judas, which was guide to them that took Jesus." We have something more here:

But thou, O LORD, be merciful unto me, and raise me up, that I may requite them [Ps. 41:10].

This verse is a reference to the resurrection of the Lord Jesus Christ. "Raise me up, that I may recompense them." In this Genesis section we have seen the death of Christ and His resurrection as well. But I want to make something startlingly clear: The death of Christ saves no one; it is the death and resurrection of Christ that saves. Paul explicitly defines the gospel in 1 Corinthians 15:3–4: "For I delivered unto you first of all that which I also received, how that Christ died for our sins according to the scriptures; And that he was buried, and that he rose again the third day according to the scriptures." Without the resurrection of the Lord there is no gospel.

Almost everyone has an opinion about the Lord Jesus. Jesus asked His disciples, ". . . Whom do men say that I the Son of man am? And they said, Some say that thou art John the Baptist: some, Elias; and others, Jeremias, or one of the prophets. He saith unto them, But whom say ye that I am? And Simon Peter answered and said, Thou art the Christ, the Son of the living God" (Matt. 16:13–16). Who do you say that Christ is? Many modern plays about Jesus leave Him on the cross or in the tomb. Thomas Jefferson left Him in the tomb in his moral teachings about Jesus. He concluded his book with a stone closing the tomb. There is no gospel there. That stone was rolled away and the Lord left the tomb. He was raised from the dead.

Because of the resurrection we can say:

Blessed be the LORD God of Israel from everlasting, and to everlasting. Amen, and Amen [Ps. 41:13].

This verse ends with a double amen. "Amen, and Amen" means that God put the finishing touches on our salvation when Christ rose from the dead, ascended into heaven, and sat down at the right hand of the throne of God. Christ finished the work of salvation for us. You don't have to add anything to it, but don't take away from the gospel by omitting the Resurrection. Without that there is no gospel.

This is the final psalm in the Genesis section. It has been well stated that the Book of Genesis is the entire Bible in miniature; that is, all the great truths of Scripture are germinal in Genesis. This first section of psalms covers the entire Book of Psalms in the same way. While the Book of Genesis concludes with a "coffin in Egypt," this Genesis section of Psalms closes on the high note of resurrection.

BIBLIOGRAPHY
(Recommended for Further Study)

Alexander, J. A. *The Psalms*. 1864. Reprint. Grand Rapids, Michigan: Zondervan Publishing House, 1964.

Gaebelein, Arno C. *The Annotated Bible*. 1917. Reprint. Neptune, New Jersey: Loizeaux Brothers, 1970.

Gaebelein, Arno C. *The Book of Psalms*. 1939. Reprint. Neptune, New Jersey: Loizeaux Brothers, 1965. (The finest prophetical interpretation of the Psalms)

Grant, F. W. *The Psalms*. Neptune, New Jersey: Loizeaux Brothers, 1895. (Numerical Bible)

Gray, James M. *Synthetic Bible Studies*. Old Tappan, New Jersey: Fleming H. Revell Co., 1906.

Ironside, H. A. *The Psalms*. Neptune, New Jersey: Loizeaux Brothers, n.d.

Jamieson, Robert; Fausset, A. R.; and Brown, D. *Commentary on the Bible*. 3 vols. Grand Rapids, Michigan: Wm. B. Eerdmans Publishing Co., 1945.

Jensen, Irving L. *The Psalms*. Chicago, Illinois: Moody Press, 1970. (A self-study guide)

Morgan, G. Campbell. *Notes on the Psalms*. Old Tappan, New Jersey: Fleming H. Revell Co., 1947.

Olson, Erling C. *Meditations in the Psalms*. Neptune, New Jersey: Loizeaux Brothers, 1939. (Devotional)

Perowne, J. J. Stewart. *The Book of Psalms*. 1882. Reprint. Grand Rapids, Michigan: Zondervan Publishing House, 1976.

Sauer, Erich. *The Dawn of World Redemption*. Grand Rapids, Michigan: Wm. B. Eerdmans Publishing Co., 1951. (An excellent Old Testament survey)

Scroggie, W. Graham. *The Psalms.* Old Tappan, New Jersey: Fleming H. Revell Co., 1948. (Excellent)

Scroggie, W. Graham. *The Unfolding Drama of Redemption.* Grand Rapids, Michigan: Zondervan Publishing House, 1970. (An excellent survey and outline of the Old Testament)

Spurgeon, Charles Haddon. *The Treasury of David.* 3 vols. Reprint. Grand Rapids, Michigan: Zondervan Publishing House, 1974. (A classic work and very comprehensive)

Unger, Merrill F. *Unger's Bible Handbook.* Chicago, Illinois: Moody Press, 1966. (A basic tool for every Christian's library)

Unger, Merrill F. *Unger's Commentary on the Old Testament.* Vol. 1. Chicago, Illinois: Moody Press, 1981. (A fine summary of each paragraph. Highly recommended)